OM
THE SELF WITHIN

A Spiritual Journey of Discovering Purpose Through Pain

Natalie Antoinette

OM: THE SELF WITHIN Copyright 2020 by Natalie Antoinette.

All rights reserved.

No part of this publication may be reproduced, distributed, or transmitted in any form or by any means, including photocopying, recording, or other electronic or mechanical methods, without the prior written permission of the publisher, except in the case of brief quotations embodied in critical reviews and certain other noncommercial uses permitted by copyright law. For permission requests, write to the publisher, addressed "Attention: Permissions Coordinator," 500 N. Michigan Avenue, Suite #600, Chicago, IL 60611.

13th & Joan books may be purchased for educational, business or sales promotional use. For information, please email the Sales Department at sales@13thandjoan.com.

Printed in the U.S. A.

First Printing, December 2021

Library of Congress Cataloging-in-Publication Data has been applied for.

ISBN: 978-1-953156-23-5

Table
OF CONTENTS

Prologue 5
Introduction 7

1: Shabdkosh 11
2: Dristi 19
3: Aparigraha 23
4: Satya 27
5: Avidya 31
6: Manas 39
7: Yajnah 47
8: Pranayama 55
9: Saucha 61
10: Buddhi 65
11: Santosha 69
12: Pratyahara 77
13: Ahimsa 85
14: Brahmacharya 91

15: OM 97

16: Kshama 109

17: Dhanya Vad 119

18: Karuna Hu 129

19: Dharnana 135

20: Amadhi 145

Epilogue 151
Bonus 157

Prologue

I WANT TO TELL you a short story. I learned about this in yoga teacher training years ago. It's the story of Ganesha. (I'm sure you have seen the elephant with fancy headgear and four arms sitting Indian-style somewhere). Yes, him!

There was a goddess named Parvati. Taking baths was her "thing." She would typically have her husband guard the door so she could bathe in peace. Can you imagine? Having a guard protect you while you had good quality self-care time. My children would rip right through those guys.

But back to the story at hand. Her husband had to take a long trip.

Once while she was taking a bath, she took turmeric paste and created a human form. She breathed life into the paste and her son was born. (Boy, do I wish it really worked like that!)

Anyway, Parvati created Ganesha to guard her door as she bathed. He was instructed not to let anyone in during this time. As Parvati bathed one night (because clearly, that's all she did), her husband, Shiva, returned from the trip. He tried to enter Parvati's chamber, but Ganesha wouldn't allow it. Shiva insisted that this was his home and demanded entry. Ganesha would not budge. He did not understand how another man was allowed to enter the chambers. Ego!

Shiva was not accustomed to being disobeyed, so he became furious. His ego got the best of him, and in his anger, he beheaded the boy.

When Parvati emerged, she was very upset to find Ganesha beheaded and explained to Shiva that this was *their* son. Shiva realized his mistake and sent his men to find a replacement for the missing head. He instructed them to take the head of the first creature they found, which turned out to be an elephant. Shiva placed the head on the boy's body and breathed life back into it.

Ganesha was then blessed as Shiva's son and leader of all groups of beings. Shiva also declared Ganesha would be honored first from then on. He is found in front of many temples, guarding the gates.

....

At first glance, this story just seems like a tale that we might tell our children or a myth without any real substance. But it's true mystical meaning really stuck with me.

Genesha was a loyal son. He stood by his mother and did what he was told. Living in ego, he could not let another man in, his opposer did not like being told *No*, and as a result, he quite literally removed Ganesha's head. This actually symbolizes the "chopping off the head of the ego." Think about it: for any type of growth to occur, what is the first thing to go? The ego.

When the ego dies, the external world, which depends on the ego for its existence, disappears along with it.

Shiva restoring life to Ganesha and replacing his head with an elephant's meant that we no longer identify with the limited individual self, but rather with the large universal Self. In this way, our life is renewed, becoming one that can truly benefit creation. He gained wisdom, compassion, and power.

Ganesha is known as the Remover of Obstacles and the Lord of Beginnings. As he stomps through the jungle, or wherever elephants live, he tears down any "debris" in the way, and obstacles are removed. In other words, Ganesha helps guide believers down new paths. He provides prosperity and success.

It's amazing what can happen when the ego is removed.

Introduction

Before I continue with a story about my real life, a story of a woman who was also beheaded—metaphorically, of course—and had to unlearn everything she thought she knew about her life to discover the real meaning of self-love, prosperity and success, I'd like to explain how this book will help you make your own.

I'm going to show you a path and process that will allow you to adopt success habits to stick with. You don't have to flip your world upside down or try to force "new habits" overnight that disrupt life and ultimately cause you to fall back into your old ways. Rather, you can make very minor, barely noticeable, changes to your daily routine and the things that don't serve you that will create that path of abundance. I hope that this book will show you that it doesn't matter who you are or where you come from; the habits, principles, and recipes in the upcoming chapters will give you a competitive edge, catapulting you to the next level.

So while this book's main focus is on spiritual success, the methods I'll share can also propel you to new levels of fulfillment in the other areas of your life, including financials, family, parenting, friendships, love, passion, intimacy, and so much more.

And that's what I love about yoga. You learn the discipline and the character of self on the mat, but the real beauty begins when you apply the lessons off the mat too.

Please note: Although we may reference Sanskrit quite often in this book, I am not Hindu. I am not Christian either, or Jewish for that matter. I hold no religion as I realize that I am a spiritual being interconnected with everything around me and something way bigger than me. So please read this book from a spiritual place, not your religious mindset. You will see that the framework of who we ALL are and what we ALL believe comes down to the core value: Being one!

So take what resonates with you and leave the rest. But whatever you do, love yourself enough to take the journey!

Let's Begin!

- OM: THE SELF WITHIN -

*"A story has no beginning or end:
arbitrarily one chooses that moment of experience from
which to look back or from which to look ahead."*

- Graham Greene -

1

Shabdkosh

THE BEGINNING

BOOM! BOOM! BOOM! A loud sound startled me as I placed the butter into the hot frying pan. Homemade caramel French toast with fresh cut strawberries was on today's breakfast menu.

"Who the hell is that?" I began to say, confused as to which friend had lost their mind at 10:06 that sunny Thursday morning. Friends popping up unannounced had been known to happen a time or two. Before I could even finish my sentence, I poked my head around the corner. Simultaneously, David, my husband, yelled "Oh, shit!" and rushed past me toward the stairwell. Not before eight armed men, each with a .45 handgun or semi-automatic and heavy body armor burst the hinges of our front door. I stood frozen in an eerie silence trying to comprehend what was happening before my eyes. It appeared the officers were yelling something in what looked like slow motion; however, there was no sound resonating from their mouths. I must have been standing there at least five minutes because I could see about five more men moving from around the side of my house, each with rifles. I realized I was only there three seconds tops as I instantly snapped back to reality when my three-year-old screeched in fear from the living room. Without thought for the five semi-automatics pointing my way demanding I "GET DOWN ON THE FUCKING GROUND RIGHT NOW," I ran for the living room. It was an uncalculated move on my part, being a Black person in America, where getting killed by the police is a growing trend; but in that moment, my only thought was to *Get to my children*, which is a natural and understandable reaction from a mother who feels her cub is in danger. Or so I thought!

POW! A single shot fired, and once again, I was met with the eerie silence, but this time, there was complete darkness.

Who knew that today would be the day that changed our lives forever....

TWO WEEKS EARLIER

The 4 am alarm sounded and it was time to start the day once again. I rolled over on the California king bed to find my phone, annoyed that David was unaffected by the sound. I dared not hit the snooze button this time because the store was supposed to be open by 4:30am or we would be subject to a $500 fine, an error we could not afford. After so many fines, you are subject to lose your contract, and we were already in jeopardy. I own a luxury wellness tea shop in BWI Airport.

This has its pros and cons; the traffic of this always busy location was a major plus. Being open for twenty hours a day, seven days a week was the biggest con.

Reluctantly, I got up, knowing that the earliest I could possibly arrive would be 5am. I started my hot water and quickly made my way to the bathroom. Thirty minutes later, I was heading out the door into the frisky October air, loading my laptop case into my X3 BMW. I hit record time pulling into the airport employee parking lot only fourteen minutes later, sparing barely enough time to push through the chaos of TSA, who seems to treat employees worse than they treat passengers. With two minutes to spare, I flicked the lights on to New Secrets Tea, my home away from home. The hustle and bustle of the airport was already in full effect, and as I pulled my laptop out while greeting the incoming customers, I already knew what today was going to bring.

Another mundane Monday. We had been at the airport for over a year, and financially, the business was thriving. The problem was not in the money but in the work it took to make that money. In just a short span, I had been able to take the business from about $12,000 a year to over $250,000. The workload that came with that increase was tremendous, and at this point, I was more than burnt out. Sometimes, because finding adequate help in this new age generation is extremely difficult, shifts were the whole twenty hours. Now, if we are to be honest, those days particularly as 'the boss' may have been shortened to 15-17 hours depending on traffic flow. However, once I got home, it was straight to the lab to create the inventory we had just spent all day getting rid of. Thankfully, David had left his corporate gig as an engineer just the year prior to join us full time as our tech guy, taking online sales to new heights. My mother, Thelma, was on board as well, using her personality skills to sell her ass off. But even with the three of us, the workload was too great. They too were overwhelmed, and since neither dreamed of spending days slaving away for a job that apparently doesn't allow for vacation or sick days, their hours of needed overtime had begun to dwindle, leaving me to pick up all the slack. I was used to it by now: wake up, go to work, come home, kiss and bathe the babies while hubby cooks dinner, force myself to eat the dinner while thinking of new ways to accomplish things more efficiently, put the babies to bed, and hit the lab to make more tea. By this time, I was on autopilot, only going to sleep with about three maybe four hours to spare before the vicious cycle started again.

Needless to say, my marriage was suffering. We had been together ten years now and just happened to get married about five months before in May. But thanks to my ambitious ways, we were heading down the road of divorce, and fast!

If you were to ask me, money was not my motive at all. I had fifteen nieces and nephews, a two-year-old and a three-year-old, all of whom were not allowed the opportunity to explore what their hearts desired. The way our family was set up, we had been known to produce many beautiful faces, but the financial support to carry such a load had never really been met. Call it an unfortunate series of circumstances, but it had been a goal of mine to provide for them the things I did not get the chance to experience. In addition, my mother should have retired by now but couldn't because she'd spent most of her life sacrificing for others instead of looking out for herself. Furthermore, my husband put his neck on the line and left his high paying job, against his family's wishes, to support the dreams of his overzealous wife. So honestly, family has always been the motive, but from the outside looking in, one might have thought otherwise.

On the random days I came home before the sunset, I was greeted by a half-enthused husband and two kisses to the mouth, and today was no different. As I kicked off my heels from the short ten-hour day, kneeling down to give our son loads of kisses, David greeted me as usual with a "Hey, baby."

Michael, our two-year-old son, was happy to see me, running to the door with open arms. Michelle, our three-year-old daughter, on the other hand, was too preoccupied with her father's iPhone to even acknowledge me. She wasn't even a teen yet and the technology struggle had started.

"Well, hello, Michelle!"

Without even turning her head from the screen, she replied, "Hi, Umi."

Removing the screen from her face, I asked, "Where is my hug? And are you watching ABCs?"

She responded by letting out a sigh to inform me I was annoying her and proceeded to scroll to her ABCs on YouTube. There was a small piece of me that wanted to chuckle, but I couldn't afford to let that show. Any ounce of weakness shown to these little one leads to a series of un-obeyed commands and a spanking.

"Any shipments today?" I asked David as I immediately got back into work mode.

"Yes ... some bottles and infusers."

As I entered the lab, I saw that the big brown boxes had already been opened. David brought in the packages and set it up in a way that I could unload inventory pretty swiftly. He seemed to be in a pretty good mood today and even offered to knock out some inventory with me, and I didn't question why this mood had occurred.

It was Thursday, the sun was shining, and I was home early because it was a busy weekend ahead—plus we were low on inventory. Usually moments like this led to all-nighters, so I took him up on his offer. I knocked out the special orders first, with which Michelle was ecstatic to help. She was never really far from me whenever I was home, often watching my every move. I always noticed it, but sometimes had to ignore it, including her, due to lack of time. Whenever workload was high and time was short, which seemed to be a lot lately, I would encourage Michael and Michelle to occupy each other. I didn't ever want them to feel rejected, so if asked, I would stop and play hide and seek or tag for maybe five minutes.

It was quickly concluded once I caught a glimpse of the lengthy to-do list on my whiteboard. I thought I was doing a pretty good job balancing motherhood and business until my daughter happened to illustrate an impression of me.

Once while the two were playing and I curated inventory, Michelle sat at the desk with a toy remote to her ear, play typing on my laptop and grooving to imaginary music. Michael walked up to her and said something in baby talk, and she replied, "Hold on a second, baby. I don't have time right now."

Unfortunately that was a line I used often in 2018: "I don't have time." Looking back now, they are words I wish I hadn't said.

The night proceeded pretty routinely. We blasted "Sade and Teyana Taylor" loud from our speakers knocking out inventory and stopped only for dance breaks, cooking, or tending to the babies. Per usual, before the night was up, we had anywhere from one to several visits. Our house, as told to us, was a safe haven for most. The atmosphere provided comfort, although I think that had a lot to do with the food and/or drinks that were always provided. Either way, our poetic friend was the visitor tonight. The babies were all tired out at this point and sound asleep in bed. Junie and David were in the sunroom playing the guitar and reciting her new lyrics for her upcoming performance with Dougie Fresh. Once everything was settled inside, I joined them for a cypher.

I didn't do it often, but I enjoyed cyphers because it was a time we would discuss world problems and how to solve them. If we couldn't cure the world that day, we discussed our problems and tried to fix those.

Either way, we were peaceful, productive, and even if just for the moment, stress-free.

We sat in our sunroom. One side was the meditation area decorated with yoga mats and a massive Buddha head; on the other side was the blue futon where Junie and David sat, two side tables, and an electric fireplace that warmed the room to a comfortable seventy-five degrees on a cold fall night. The white Christmas lights that dangled all year round provided a starry vibe against the night sky. I joined them Indian-style on the fur rug, waiting for David to finish rolling the spliff in the raw papers. We listened to two of Junie's new hits and critiqued. It was always fun being first to hear the songs before they hit the airwaves. It was one of the many privileges we were honored to have. Forty-five minutes and two cups of tea later, we said our goodbyes to Junie and re-entered the house. David immediately retreated to the master bedroom with his Nintendo switch in hand and I, to the lab to bottle up the last flavor for the night. Another thirty minutes and it was right into a deep sleep.

That following Tuesday, David and I had planned a date night. The morning started as usual, up early and off to the airport. I was back by 10 a.m. because I needed to get a lot of administrative things done. Everyone in the house was just beginning to wake up, so I began to prepare breakfast, peach oatmeal and scrambled eggs with a berry smoothie. We spent time talking about the day and enjoying family time at the table before the children departed to brush their teeth and do their learning time. I had a lot of computer work to complete this morning, and if any 'date' was going to take place that night, I had to get cracking, so I allowed ABC learning time to take place in front of the TV. While David set things up, I got the babies dressed in their day clothes. Pulling her shirt over Michelle's head, I began their routine questions.

"Did you have a good sleep?"

"Yes, I did."

"Well, did you dream?"

"Actually-" a phrase that caught me by surprise every time her little mouth turned up to say it.

"I did ... I dreamed that lots of men came into our house with guns for Baba."

Our children did not call us Mom and Dad, but Umi and Baba, which means mother and father of life in Amharic.

"Oh really...well that's interesting, mama."

David and I caught a glance at each other and smiled at how amazing this little soul was. I didn't think anything of it.

Strike 1!

"If you want to be happy, do not dwell in the past, do not worry about the future, focus on living fully in the present."

- Roy T. Bennett -

2

Dristi

THE FOCUS OF THE EYE

LATER THAT NIGHT, Granna intervened and picked up her grandbabies after work. She was a local pastor at her nearby church, so it was a swift stop pass. Once the babies were gone, the pre-gaming began. He would roll one, I'd pour up the drinks and cut up some limes, music would play, and we would spend about an hour or so weaving around each other getting ready.

This seemed to be the only time we actually liked each other. Business was done for the day, and the children were out for the night, so we could actually notice each other. David stood about six feet three inches, slender build with lean muscle in all the right places, his caramel brown skin glistening fresh out of the shower as he stood ironing his shirt, wrapped in only a towel. I passed him his Bombay sapphire and ginger ale with lime, and he grabbed both the drink and my hand to pull me closer. We were pelvis to pelvis, and as I looked into his bright hazel eyes and big pearly white teeth, I was reminded why we'd gotten together in the first place. It was moments like this that kept us alive—only problem was, nowadays they were few and far between. David resembled Bow Wow, and his conversation was always on the next level. It made it easy to be attracted to him, and I wasn't the only one who thought so.

I'm sure many of the women who called him for whatever reason or came by to visit, with or without my presence, thought the same thing.

There are a lot of family members who felt like I was too open to allowing beautiful women around him when I wasn't around, but I trusted David. I knew that no matter what woman threw their body his way, he had enough respect for me to dodge that bullet. I was his and he was mine, and with nights like this, nothing could come between that.

We didn't actually have anything planned for the night, so I put on a fitted mauve T-shirt dress, some distressed blue jeans, and my black suede thigh highs. We took a puff of the spliff for the road, I sprayed my Prada perfume to mask any smell of mary jane, and we got into his blue convertible Mustang. The night was a little chilly, but not too cold that we couldn't drop the top and blast the heat. We cruised through the city trying to figure out where to go. I simply enjoyed being out and caught myself sticking my hands up to feel the air dance around my fingers. Our first stop was at a local Mexican joint. After all, it was Taco Tuesday!

About four shrimp, two fish, three beef, three steak tacos and five margaritas later, we were well satisfied and off to our next destination. Drunk bowling seemed to be the move because, well, we were running out of places to go at 9:30 on a Tuesday night. The movies were an option, but not a good one, because we knew we both would be asleep before the previews were even over. If you let me tell you, I let him win, 116 to 89. My competitive nature didn't bother me, but anything for a little ass grab or a squeeze. Don't get me wrong; I enjoyed the bowling game but was more interested in the game we could play later. The lights went out at Rock and Roll, and we were last to leave the parking lot. We were only ten minutes from home at this time, so I decided it was time to start the real fun.

We teased each other on the way home, barely stopping at any red lights. Whipping into the driveway, we stumbled to the doorway. A trail of clothes led to the bedroom. Starting slow, I rode him like it was the last time—little did I know it would be. We made sweet passionate love. I was almost certain I heard a wolf howl in the near distance.

- OM: THE SELF WITHIN -

"Abundance is not something we receive externally. It's something we tune in to from within"

- NatalieAntoinette -

3

Aparigraha

TRUST AND SHARE IN ABUNDANCE

*I*T WAS FRIDAY, and once again I was opening the doors to New Secrets Tea. I would only be here a few short hours. I really needed an assistant so from 10am - 2pm, I would be conducting interviews to fulfill that much-needed position. I vetted about eight prospects before making my decision. After calling and hiring Donna that day, I informed her she would have all her paperwork in an email by 5pm, and training would start Monday. I finished up a few things at the shop and rolled out about 2:30pm. Heading home, doing 75-80 mph the whole way, I sang at the top of my lungs. I felt happy. I would finally have an extra pair of hands. This would allow us to take the business up a notch, and more importantly, I could do more around the house as a wife and mother. A complaint I had heard all too often. Maybe I could salvage this relationship.

I turned into the neighborhood and instantly thought *What the hell is going on now?* as I turned down the music.

There were about five cars in our driveway, but none were David's.

Where is he? Who is here now? Making sure not to ruin my mood, I found a spot in the neighbor's front yard and proceeded to my house with caution. I wasn't scared or nervous because it was the new norm; I was just curious. Big Boy greeted me at the door with a huge smile and a bigger bear hug. Instantly I knew everything was all good. Big Boy was one of David's friends. I hadn't known him long personally, but he always treated me and the house with respect, and I was big on that. Plus, David had obviously told him where the spare key was, and if David trusts you, I trust you.

I entered my home and there were seven smiling faces. They all were without shoes, so I didn't need to curse anyone out; Big Boy knew the house rules. Before I could get to any questions, Black, who was on FaceTime, was handed to me.

"Newnew, beautiful ... How are you?"

Side-eyeing him, I replied, "I'm fine, Black ... and you?"

Black and I had an unspoken love/hate relationship. He was a slick talker, and he knew I knew that. I was the only one he couldn't fast-talk. He respected it and hated it all in one. David and Black go way back to children's church. Childhood friends are always fun to have, but something just didn't sit well with me about Black. However, he was David's friend, and I was personally asked to play nice when it came to him. So, per my husband's request, I followed up with, "What's going on in here and where's David?" in a friendly, matter-of-fact kind of way

"He said he's on his way. We just ordered some stuff and had to get it asap. Plus we ain't wanna leave nothing on your porch."

"Uh huh. You lucky they got their shoes off."

I passed the phone back to Big Boy, greeting everyone with a hug, and proceeded to walk to my room.

Strike 2.

- OM: THE SELF WITHIN -

"Some days are not as beautiful and some nights not as wonderful, you need to be careful not to worry about the hurtful things of life, just focus on what is meaningful."

- Gift Gugu Mona -

4

Satya
TO TELL THE TRUTH

The weekend passed, and the same activities took place. I was scheduled for a show next weekend, so I would spend most, if not all, of this weekend giving the other employees a break. Shows usually meant leaving town from Thursday to Sunday as a pop-up shop. These were our money-making times, so I needed to be well prepared. A lot of inventory was to be made to survive the weekend away, plus I would need to stock the airport before I left. This upcoming show was super important because in less than three weeks, we were scheduled to open our second location. The money made this weekend was going to furnish our tea shop in the up-and-coming Remington area. It's the new gentrified spot of Baltimore, which means a lot of money was being poured into that area. It also meant business would boom. We are excited about this move because it would ultimately mean more freedom. More work but more freedom, if that makes any sense.

Over the next three days, packages would be rolling because I had ordered tons of bottles, herbs, and infusers. Once the herbs arrived, I could begin the process.

Each flavor now held a recipe. Make the tea in large batches, place them in individual bags, seal the bags, fill the containers with the appropriate amount of tea bags, label and seal the bottles. This seemingly simple process could take about three to five hours per flavor, and there were about eleven flavors to work on. Needless to say, I had a lot to get done. When I arrived home Monday evening, two of the six packages had already arrived and were awaiting me in the lab. Trying not to be overwhelmed by the daunting task ahead, I greeted the family and decided that sitting with the family for dinner that night might not have been a wise decision. I was already exhausted from the fourteen-hour day but knew I couldn't allow that thought to process because I had too much to do.

"Your food is in the microwave if you're hungry."

"Thank you, baby. I will eat it in a minute. You up for helping me tonight?"

"Nah, you got that."

He grabbed the Nintendo switch and headed to the sunroom for a blunt. About twenty minutes later, he retreated to the bedroom with his iPhone in hand. Another five minutes passed, and I noticed the iPhone light was still on, which meant he couldn't be sleep. Now... maybe I should have left it alone, but the irritation took over, and suddenly I couldn't think straight.

Walking to the bedroom, I stood in the door. "Why can't you help me again?" I asked.

He picked up the sarcasm in my voice. "Because I don't want to, and I'm tired."

With an eye roll, I replied, "But I want to, and I'm not tired? Would it kill you to suck it up and help me?"

"Oh, here you go. Would it kill you to come home, cook, and suck a little dick?"

I wasn't expecting that response, but I was not at all surprised. David had often complained I put the business before the family. I'd never agreed with this statement, but I will say that there were days I found it hard to play 'business owner' and come home and be 'wife' and 'mommy' when I could barely keep my eyes open. Could I have balanced a little bit better? Maybe! Would I have been able to balance better with more help? I'd like to think so. Either way, I was too tired to not be offended by the response.

"Are you serious right now? I would love to do all of the above, but I have a lot of things to do and very little time to do it. Maybe if you got off your ass and helped, I'd have energy to do so!"

"Yeah, right! This is your business, not mine! I've made more than enough sacrifices for you, and all you do is stress. Women should want their man to provide for them, and you sit down and care for the house and kids."

I was annoyed we were once again discussing what *women* want. David came from a very stable family, and me, not so much. He often made claims that insinuated all women want the same thing. It caused a lot of arguments because my response would always demand he stop trying to categorize me with all women ... other women ... women in his family.

"It's *our* business when it's all good, but *my* business when it's grind time, huh? And stop with the all women business. I'm not built like that, but you already knew that, or you shouldn't have married me."

"You got that right." His quiet but sharp reply went straight to my chest.

How did I get here? I thought. One of my biggest fears in life was to have to get a divorce and have my children grow up like me. I prided myself on never being a woman to pressure a man to be with, let alone marry, me. Maybe that's why we'd gone ten years before getting married.

Yet here I was, standing face to face with it, and I wasn't sure I would win. Where was the gentleman I once knew, who laughed at all my jokes and dreamed bigger than I did? Before me stood a man who had all the answers, fought with a sharp tongue, and was never wrong. At that moment, I really missed my friend, and as I looked into David's stern eyes, I could see he was nowhere to be found. It hurt, but I couldn't let it show.

"Wow" was all I could muster up. "Never mind."

Fighting back tears, I swallowed the golf ball in my throat and stormed back into the lab. When the coast was clear, I shed one tear. By time the water droplet hit the table, my sadness turned into frustration, frustration to anger, and anger into indifference. I plugged in my headset and blasted "Lauryn Hill Miseducation" until I finished the last tea bag.

"The highest form of ignorance happens when you reject something you know nothing about"

- NatalieAntoinette -

Avidya

IGNORANCE:
THE ROOT CAUSE OF SUFFERING

David and I didn't say much the next two days. He did his work, which I was specifically asked to stay out of, and I did mine. Wednesday night rolled around, and I had less than twelve hours to bottle, label, and seal the remainder of the inventory. I'd started days ago, but somehow I always ended up pulling an all-nighter the night before. Tonight would be no different. I finally called it a night around 4:30am.

֍

I got up that Thursday morning around 8am, with absolutely no clue that two hours from now, my world would change. I started boxing all the work I'd completed overnight. I would need to make sure I had everything before David was asked to load the truck. Both my son and daughter came dashing down the stairs around 9:15ish, and I knew I didn't have long before they would be asking for food. I turned on their ABCs on the TV to buy me another hour or so. As I stacked the outgoing boxes by the couch to be taken outside, I heard the UPS truck pull up and called for David. He rushed out the door to receive the package. I caught a glimpse of the delivery man. He was a White male with dark brown hair and piercing blue eyes. Not our normal delivery guy, but hey, everyone deserves a day off right!

He tilted his hat as he re-entered his truck, and David came smiling into the house.

"Is that my teacups?" I asked, entering the kitchen to start breakfast. The children had stolen grapes from the fridge and were devouring the whole bag, so I knew I couldn't put it off any longer. I waited for a response while reaching for the butter and collecting the frying pan. My response didn't come immediately because at just that moment David's FaceTime rang. Black was on the other end.

"Everything good, my brother?"

"Yeah man, the package is here!"

What are these two up to now? I thought to myself as I prepared the French toast butter.

"Anything different about the delivery guy?" Black asked, which sounded odd to me but was quickly dismissed when I dropped a whole strawberry on the floor.

"Nah, all good." They spoke a little more, but David stepped into the sunroom so I couldn't hear. About two minutes later, he returned, and I heard him cutting open the box.

♩

Boom The gun fired, and it wasn't until I opened my eyes that I realized I wasn't hit. The bullet hole was in my wall, chest range right in front of me. I threw my hands in the air and began to yell, but my feet would not stop. I was terrified that my children were going to witness the death of their mother, and yet my feet would not stop.

Protect your cubs.

Once the sound returned, I heard myself saying, "I will not get on the floor. Put the fucking gun down in front of my children. Put the fucking gun down! Get the gun out of my child's face. Put the fucking gun down!"

I was yelling this to the officer who had his semi automatic pointed right at my three-year-old, who was currently screaming her head off. My son, God bless his heart, looked at the men and then back to the TV. His favorite part of Daniel Tiger was playing, plus he'd already won because he had the whole bag of grapes. Victory was his, and nobody could stop that. I heard the officer cock his gun again, telling me to get down for the last time.

With fear in my eyes and rage in my heart, I said the only thing I could think of. "No!"

Preparing to die, I turned my back to the officers and cuddled the babies, wrapping them both into a bear hug and out of range of the army of policemen swarming through the door. I dropped to one knee, stroked my baby girl's face, and told her it was going to be okay because "Umi got you." I hugged them again and took what I thought was my last breath, saying, "God protect my babies!"

I was in this position for about two minutes as each officer ran through the house yelling, "CLEAR… CLEAR… CLEAR."

David was cuffed, seated in the lab across the hall. I could see the shame on his face. I remember standing up to seat the babies on the couch when I realized God himself must have been present that morning. Just then, for no reason at all other than wanting to stop by, my mother's Escalade pulled up. Of course they wouldn't let her in. But they followed me around the house as I quickly prepared an overnight bag and got them dressed to leave. Thank God she'd showed!

As I was putting their coats on, one officer made light of the situation by attempting to entertain them with Elmo's voice. If I must say, he was rather good but my anger wouldn't allow me to crack a smile. Once ready, Officer Stan extended his hand, which I quickly rejected.

"I will walk them out myself," I spat.

"You can't leave the house."

Not thinking, I stated, "Neither my children nor I trust you. Less than five minutes ago, you broke my door, yelling, and pointing a gun at our faces. I will be walking them to the car. If you feel inclined, you can accompany me, and if I run, feel free to shoot me in the back. But I WILL be walking MY CHILDREN to my MOTHER'S CAR!" I pointed to it.

I think he heard the seriousness in my voice because when I pushed past him, I was met with no resistance. I had won a small victory. I loaded them into the car and gave them a kiss.

"Umi will be back tonight to pick you up, okay? Be good for Grandma, and I will see you soon. Thank you for being so brave today. I love you!"

Thelma was standing in the car doorway when I closed it.

"What the hell?"

I cut her off. "Your guess is as good as mine, I have no fucking clue, and I'm not inside right now. They broke the damn hinges on the door. Who pays for that shit? They could have knocked, and I would have opened the fucking door!"

My mother is Jamaican. If you know anything about Caribbean mothers, you know they don't care who you are or how old; if you are disrespectful, prepared to get a smack to the head. So I normally don't swear in front of my mother, but in light of the situation, she made an exception.

" The inventory for tonight's show is lined up against the couch. Just in case, my email has all the information."

I returned to work mode because I was scheduled to hit the road in about three hours.

"Contact Donna. She has all the information."

I kissed my mother goodbye as Officer Stan signaled me back in. Donna had been given about fifteen hours of training since Monday and had access to all my files. I would take care of the rest tomorrow. I re-entered the house and was instructed to take a seat next to David, who was now cuffed and seated on the living room sofa.

"I'm so sorry." David looked over to me with pitiful eyes.

Not really understanding what was happening, I gave him a head nod and looked up to see the same piercing blue eyes from before. At that moment I recognized who it was. Officer Thomas had been the UPS delivery guy from earlier. My heart sank to my stomach as I quickly began to put two and two together.

I turned to David. "What exactly are you sorry for? What the fuck is going on, David?"

His response was interrupted by another White man, this time in a suit, who had clearly just arrived. "I'm Detective Dan. This here is a search and seizure warrant signed by a judge. This morning around 10 o'clock a package was delivered. It was detected at the UPS by a search dog to contain CDS [controlled drug substance]. It was searched at the warehouse and confirmed that fifteen pounds of substance resembling marijuana was sealed in the package ..."

Sidenote: Let's be clear. I knew that he smoked weed. Who doesn't? I also knew that he sold some to close friends here and there. I mean think about it. Has weed really ever hurt anybody?

I also knew that we had registered guns in the house. We did live in the city with two children. Protection is necessary! Better to be prepared and never need it than not prepared at all.

I know we are not thugs, but there were five White males quite literally staring down at two African American bodies. We were tax-paying citizens, causing no harm, building communities and trying to survive this thing called American Life, yet something told me... they didn't see that.

His voice began to trail off as I sat there.

I could once again see mouths moving but could not hear anything. All the blood had left my face, and all I could hear was the sound of my own heartbeat. I looked over to Officer Thomas, who stood watching us like a hound dog, his eyes still cutting through my soul. I will never forget those eyes.

When I finally tuned back in, David was mentioning locations in our house. Each time he named a spot, an officer would go and retrieve more pounds of CDS. David was very cooperative. They asked, he gave answers. I sat amazed at the pile of drugs which was being collected into a black Tupperware bucket. I heard the officer ask about any weapons, and at this point all eleven officers were just standing and waiting. This had to be the easiest search warrant ever conducted. If there was any time I needed David to be a mind reader, it was now. *Don't answer that,* I thought.

"There are some knives in the kitchen," I cut in, hoping David would pick up on my hint. He didn't!

"Our guns are stacked away in the master bedroom. They are registered, and there are three of them."

Like I said, I knew we had guns; they were for protection. They were never used, but having children and living in the city, I didn't mind. Plus they were legal and David was no thug. Somehow, my gut said sharing this information would not be a good thing.

One of the officers whose name I did not catch saw a label in the lab.

"Hey, guys, check this out. This is the tea spot in the airport my wife loves. I brought her some not too long ago. They're across from ChickFi-lA in the Southwest terminal. You remember, Roy?"

The lead detective asked if that was true, and I confirmed. He asked whose business it was, and with pride I replied, "Mine." (Ugh.. there goes that ego!)

I should have remained quiet, but those words gave me a fleeting feeling that they might be on our side. I should have known better!

"All right, guys, let's get her cuffed and load them up."

I turned to see they were taking out five tubs of CDS and turned back wide-eyed. "I'm not going anywhere. I don't have anything to do with it. I have a show to attend, and I need to leave in the next hour."

"Yeah, please don't lock her up. She has nothing to do with anything. Just take me and let her go," David pleaded.

"This is your business, right?"

"Yes, but as he said, I have nothing to do with this."

The officer put a label in my face, and I looked down at the label that had come on this morning's package:

David and Newnew Jones

New Secrets Tea

Both my name and my business name was on the fifteen pounds of CDS that had been delivered by the feds this morning.

Strike 3 ... I'm out!

"The divine self is the author and creator of our story. But without efficient spiritual awareness, the physical self tends to rearrange the plot."

- NatalieAntoinette -

6

Manas

TO PULL INFORMATION FROM THE LOWER MIND RATHER THAN WISDOM

I WAS SICK TO my stomach. I continued to hear David pleading with the detective that I was innocent and had nothing to do with it.

The detective responded, "We will just take her down because she is over the age of eighteen. She'll be out within a couple of hours."

A little blood returned to my face. I thought, *Okay, that isn't fair but shouldn't be too bad.*

As I stood to be cuffed, I looked David in his teary eyes.

"All I need in this life of sin..."

I began quietly singing to make light of the situation. It was not at all a time to play, but I could see the shame in his face, and I just wanted him to know I was on his side. I wasn't sure what would happen to him, honestly, but I was confident that we could explain the situation to someone, and we would have it squared by nightfall. I guess he knew just how serious it all was because it looked like it caused great pain to crack the little bit of smile he did show.

I dropped my head in shame as I stepped out the door and back into the brisk sun. This time the neighborhood stood watching and whispering amongst themselves. I stepped up into the cold paddy wagon and jumped at the sound of the van door slamming behind me. The ride downtown was quiet, making one stop to pick up another individual. I sat myself in a small compartment of the vehicle. The door was pressed against my knees.

"Do you still love me?" I heard David through the cold metal.

"Of course. We just have one goal: Get back to the babies!" I was optimistic.

Don't get me wrong: I wasn't oblivious to jail or cops. I never really got on the wrong side of the law, mostly because I feared my mother more than any cop. But let's just say I knew a few stories. Plus, I wasn't like people who would get locked up. I wasn't a troublemaker. This was just a misunderstanding.

We pulled up to what I now know was Central Bookings Detention Center. When we got out, I looked around to see we were caged in. I couldn't run if I'd wanted to. Thank God I didn't want to. They led the men, now four of them, to one door and me to another. Since I wasn't being held like the others, I quickly walked over to David to give him a quick peck on the lips.

"I'll see you later." I smiled and returned to the officer, who was looking at me like I was crazy for walking away from him.

"Sorry." I smirked as I stepped into another world. Immediately the sun was gone.

I was at intake.

The walls were composed of dirty white and green cinder blocks, and there was a window where the correctional officers sat and a narrow hallway with about four cells on each side. Six ladies, some with tattoos and battle wounds, stood in pink jumpsuits before me. They halted their conversation and each stared at me from top to bottom as I was escorted past and pushed into a single cell bullpen. I shuddered when the thick iron door to my cell slammed shut behind me.

> *"Lessons learned the easy way are hard to remember, but lessons learned the hard way are never forgotten"*
>
> - NatalieAntoinette -

Worry began to sink in, but I kept chanting, *I'll be out in a few hours!'* to myself. Somehow even I didn't believe it. It took me less than a minute to examine my new environment. It was a faded waxed cement room with a steel toilet seat without toilet paper. I pleaded for a phone call but never got a response because another girl two cells down took all the attention.

"Let me the fuck out!" she repeatedly screamed as she kicked and banged on anything that would make noise.

Eventually, an irritated correctional officer kicked back. "SHUT THE FUCK UP!" That must have been what she was waiting for.

"You shut the fuck up. Let me out and I'll show you how to shut the fuck up. Let me catch you uptown."

"Bitch, I go home at 3 o'clock. How about you?" The C.O. chuckled.

She wasn't talking to me, but even I felt that one. They went back and forth for a few minutes, each comment a little sharper than the last. I began to tap my head against the wall trying not to become overwhelmed with all the emotions bubbling inside.

Why would they use my name on the package? Can they hurry up? Can they even keep me in here without proof? What is that smell? I'm going to be late! Why in the hell would he put my business name on something like that? What was he thinking? He wasn't! I hope he's okay over there!

Over the next few hours, I was forced to play musical cells, bouncing back and forth between group, single, and holding. My stomach began to grumble as I realized it was now 9pm and I hadn't eaten all day. I asked for food and was told they didn't have anything. This couldn't be right, *When are they going to release me?* My stomach turned.

I slid my arms into my shirt because it had to be about fifty degrees and curled up in a ball on the cement floor. I must have dozed off because I was startled awake by a bang on the cell door.

"Jones?"

I sat up with a smile, excited to finally be free. "Yes?"

"Come with me!"

Ugh gosh! Another cell! I thought.

It was a male CO this time, and he walked me to the front. We stopped at the cell. He told me to step into the bullpen with three other ladies, and I became confused.

"Here are your charge papers." He handed me a thick twenty-eight-page packet.

"Charge papers? I'm supposed to be going home." I was lost.

"Ha!" he replied as he slammed the door once more. This time the sound set all the way in.

I turned around to face the three women. One lady had her back against the wall, one had her face in her hands, and the last was on the toilet. I said hi and found a spot on the cold cinder block to read through my pages. I couldn't comprehend it all, but as I flipped the pages, certain words stuck out to me.

It read: "Federal package delivered fifteen pounds ... search and seizure discovered a total of seventy pounds of CDS ... two hundred fifty THC pens ... three firearms used for drug trafficking ... manufactured and distributed by New Secrets Tea ..."

My mind began to race. *Where the hell did all that weed come from? Why would they have that much? Why in my damn house? One plant is considered manufacturing? That's dumb. Why the hell did he use my name? I'm kicking somebody's ass!*

My jaw dropped. It was that moment I realized I wasn't going to be leaving tonight. I fought back tears knowing I wasn't in a place where openly crying was a good idea. All I could do now was wait to see the commissioner and hope to be freed.

More hours passed, and I still had not been fed or received a phone call. It was now 1am, and I was freezing. None of us could sleep, so we started conversing. Over the next two hours, each lady opened up to me, at first to give advice on what they thought was coming and then to reveal why each was here. They had all been down this road before and could tell I was a rookie.

"Man, I just need another hit," said girl one.

"Shittt, you got that fucking right. I was just down the strip, I just finished ... yeah ... know what I mean and before I could even hit the corner the boys rolled up on me. Fuck, man. Shit's crazy," started girl two.

"I'm just tryna get bail, but I already know I'm getting time," a cold girl three said.

"What are y'all here for? If you don't mind me asking."

By this time all three ladies began to get in a spooning position for warmth.

"A pussy charge."

"I just had a couple pills, that's all."

"Murder. Two shots to the head."

I swallowed hard as I sat upright, head pressed against the wall. Who knew I would be spending the rest of my night with a dope fiend, a prostitute and a murderer? We all closed our eyes and dozed off.

> *"You're a Diamond- Built from pressure
> and hard to break!"*
>
> - NatalieAntoinette -

It was 6am, and I was finally given a meal. It was packaged bologna with sunflower seeds and a small packet of goldfish. I was starved, so I eagerly tore open my brown boxed lunch. Putting the funny smelling meat on the bread, I popped open the packet of mayo that came with the meal. It looked and poured out like cooking oil, but I had already drenched my bread. Disgusted but hungry, I shoved the food down my throat. They provided nothing to drink, so the toilet water that ran through the sink washed it down. At this point, I was just grateful to have gotten something.

There was no way to track time, but hours later I was taken to see the commissioner. She was a Black lady around thirty-five with a banging blowout. She asked me several questions which included name, age, address. Never once did she make eye contact with me. She requested "a second to review your charges." Without any further questioning, she stated, "After reviewing your file, you'll be held with no bond."

"Wait, what?" I almost choked, like Idris Elba in his meme.

"That's my final decision. You can go!"

I was coldly dismissed, still waiting for some sort of eye contact. I just knew if she only looked at me, she would see my innocence and reconsider. It never happened, and I was distraught. As I was escorted back down the hall, I realized we were walking past the men's section. I yelled for David and to my surprise, he too was in a commissioner room, one I was walking right by. He immediately got up and pressed his hands against the window.

"What they say?" His eyes said so much more.

"No bail." I cracked another smile, feeling as though I needed to be strong for us both, but really wanting to cry.

"Listen, there is one goal: Get to our children," he said as I was being dragged away.

"I'll see you Monday."

I was put into a single cell and told to wait for the second commissioner. There was a chance that they would say something different. The officer still denied my call, saying, "No calls until after the second commissioner."

Well, that's not legal, I thought sarcastically, but what could I do but wait? The second commissioner rolled around a few hours later, and he agreed with the first because I was a 'danger to the community.' Little ol' me. The doula and yoga instructor who did community work every Sunday. 'A danger'! I had to go to bail review, a process where they determine if what the commissioner stated is correct. Either they lower the bail, increase it, or leave it the same. It all sounded a bit redundant and a waste of time, if you ask me. But nobody was asking me so.... here we were.

Fortunately this happens the very next day, so it wouldn't be long. Unfortunately, today was now Friday, so I had to wait until Monday, which meant a weekend in jail. Annoyed at this whole process, I played along, dying to see Monday.

Hanging on to the C.O.'s words, I asked for my phone call but was again denied because it was time to "change clothes."

I felt degraded being told to strip, have all my items confiscated, then I was forced to bend over and cough. I was shoved into a room no bigger than a broom closet and told to shower with cold water. Making it quick, I dried off and put on my new fit, a pink jumpsuit. They fingerprinted me and took my mugshot. It was official. I was inmate 1567214.

"Sacrifice is a part of life. It's supposed to be. It's not something to regret. It's something to aspire to."

- Mitch Albom -

Yajnah

TO SACRIFICE FOR A HIGHER PURPOSE

I MADE ONE FINAL attempt to get a phone call. Again they denied me, this time saying, "It's time to go upstairs. You can get your call then."

Naïvely, I followed, now wishing to hurry and get to a location where I could call a familiar voice and let them know I was okay but not okay. When I came off the elevator on the fifth floor, I noticed two dorms, one to the left and one to the right. I approached the three officers seated behind a desk.

"This is Jones." The escorting officer half stepped off the elevator then quickly returned.

"Can I get my phone call please?" I almost stuttered trying to get it out fast enough.

"No ma'am." One officer smiled.

Not returning the smile, I asked, "Why not?"

"We are on MSC."

"MSC?"

"Maximum security conditions."

I didn't understand, but I knew I wasn't getting that call. They didn't even care to explain. There were two inmates in the hallway who sized me up. One girl, called Troy, licked her lips and said, "Oh, she pretty ... real pretty."

The second Dom, a woman who acts and dresses very masculine, agreed. I refused to let fear show. I've seen enough "jail movies" in my life, and this seemed to be fitting the description. Besides, I only had to make it through the weekend. The lazy officers had both doms escort me to my assigned bed, which I later discovered was not my actual assigned bed. When I entered dorm B, it was a wild scene. There were about ninety-four women yelling and running amuck in this square room. Ten steel tables sat in the center of the room with about forty-five metal bunk beds on the perimeter. Six bathroom stalls with cold metal stools were at the front of the room and eight showers in the back, four on each side. The room got semi quiet as 'fresh meat' walked the runway. I made eye contact with no one, making sure to keep a poker face. They threw my mattress on a top bunk in the back, and I immediately climbed up to observe my surroundings. My heart was racing right now; the movies seemed a little safer, honestly.

"FEED UP," they called.

It was now 4:30pm, and I was getting my first meal upstairs. Meals were served on a five-part compartmentalized brown plastic tray. Tonight's meal was called "donkey dicks." They are supposed to be sausage links, but the meat remains a pink uncooked mystery, and the smell was repulsive. It was accompanied with fruit mix, canned greens, and a bland overcooked vegetable medley. I later discovered that every meal has three slices of bread with it.

I sucked up the smell and tried to take a bite, but instantly regurgitated. I don't know what it's supposed to taste like, but if I had to guess what a donkey's penis actually tasted like ... this would be it.

Needless to say, I didn't eat. I tried to remain low-key for the remainder of the weekend, only really coming from my bunk at meal time or to pee. It was the best way to avoid trouble and get to Monday. I came across the book "The Shack," which occupied my time. It was a pretty great read, if I may add, and it kept me entertained enough but allowed me to be aware of my very rambunctious surroundings.

> "If I take away consequences of people's choices, I destroy the possibility of Love. Love that is forced is no love at all"
>
> - THE SHACK

The best way to describe my experience would be 'living in a college dorm with a bunch of high schoolers.' There was a fight almost every two hours over who said what to which girlfriend or something of that nature. Since we were on MSC, all privileges were revoked, leaving ninety plus women without recreational time, phones, or a place to do anything really. It was almost a setup. Anytime a fight broke out, the problem child was pulled into the hallway a maximum of ten minutes, and then put right back. The girls acted like troubled children with no home training. Most had not even completed high school, and some of the correctional officers were no better. Shifts ran in thirds. "A" shift was from 7am-3pm, "B" shift 3pm-11pm, and "C" shift from 11pm-7am. This is really how we told the time.

On Sunday our C shift officer came in good and drunk. I found it completely inappropriate but couldn't help but find comedy in the situation.

"Here comes Ms. Hanes' ol' drunk ass again" shouted one inmate, loud enough that it drew attention.

"Yeah, yeah ... Shut the fuck up" she replied with a slow blink.

She didn't really smell of alcohol, but she definitely had a glossy look and swayed while she stood. There was no doubt she was under "somebody's" influence.

"You probably going to go drink another 40 on your break. You don't even eat. Just drink with your dumb ass." That got her riled up.

"Don't worry about what the fuck I do with your ol' dumb dyke ass. Dyke bitch."

They went tit for tat for another five minutes, and I couldn't help but release the occasional chuckle at the old school 'you ol' jokes.... classic. She eventually gave up and staggered back to her desk, where she slept for the remainder of the night.

I promise you, I'm not making this stuff up

❢

Monday morning rolled around, and we were finally off MSC. Nine o'clock hit, and the phones came on. I was finally able to place a call to my mother. My first call was thirty minutes. She was hysterical as expected but was able to pull it together long enough to figure out what to do with the babies until I got home. I instructed her on how to make sure everything would run smoothly at the airport. I would follow up after my bail review, which would be around 1pm that same day. I should be home by nightfall.

I was informed that on Thursday afternoon, the BWI officers had been alerted of the arrest and summoned the hound dogs to our store. Of course they didn't find anything, but it caused a lot of commotion and questioning. The airport was now seeking answers, and we were in jeopardy of losing our lease. Not to mention the rumors that quickly made their way around the terminals.

'This is humiliating' ran through the back of my mind as I tried to brush past it. First, we had to go meet our lawyers who would represent us at the bail review.

❢

I met with a public defender, who went over my case and my charges. He then paused and said, "I have an offer for you. If you are willing to corporate and give us names and anything else that could be helpful, you could walk away today, immune. Your husband gets 6-9 years, and you see your kids."

"But I don't know anything," I replied, frustrated that that was the only offer to get me home today.

He insisted that I give him something, anything, so he could win this case and I would go home, but I stood firm.

Now let's just pause right here. I did not know there was so much weed at the house and I for damn sure did not know my personal or business name was attached but I knew a lot more than I let on. I knew the names of everyone who would come by the house, where they lived, and I could possibly get you the head of what I've pieced together as an operation. I can give you Black.

But... come on, guys, you know the rules. ONE BAND, ONE SOUND. I know nothing. Plus we are talking about the father of my two children. He doesn't need to be in here any more than I do.

Had I given up the information, or at least what I did know, this story may have been written a little differently. I guess you can say I brought this on myself. What we are about to see is what "No Snitching" gets you.

He nodded in understanding and explained what he would ask for in the courtroom. I felt confident in how he spoke and that he would be able to get me off. He dismissed me and said he would see me later, but I didn't know that was not physically. At bail review time, we were led into a small room with about six chairs and a TV monitor that showed the courtroom. The judge entered the room and asked the public defender who he was representing. He gave the names of the two girls in the room with me but forgot mine. The judge then spoke to another attorney in the room. I couldn't see him, but I could hear.

"Hello, Mr. Brown ... who is your defendant today?"

"Hi, your honor. Give me one second. I need to check my phone!" he replied.

I shook my head, sorry for the individual who had the incompetent lawyer who didn't even know his client's name. Then Mr. Brown stepped up. "Your honor, I'm here on behalf of Newnew Jones." My eyes widened.

Shit.

I could only gasp because I just knew that wasn't going to be good. My family had hired a lawyer to represent me, which normally is a good thing, but I immediately closed my eyes and began to pray.

Brown began pleading my case in the most unconvincing way. "You know, your honor, she doesn't pose as a flight risk, and her husband is really to blame. Not to put everything on him, but I was thinking maybe a $50,000 bond?" Not even I was convinced.

"Bail is revoked." She didn't even hesitate.

I let out a small smile because, in my mind, I was already released. She'd just told me the 'no bail' I had was revoked, which meant I was free... right? Plus it's innocent until proven guilty. I looked over at the correctional officer, awaiting her approach to remove my cuffs. She didn't budge. My smile instantly dropped when I made eye contact and read her face. She wasn't moving because 'her bail is revoked' meant I was staying with no bail. I wasn't going home; I was going back upstairs. My eyes instantly began to water.

When the elevator doors opened on the fifth floor and I got a whiff of the urine smell in the hallway, I lost it. Tears began to pour down my face as I searched for my breath.

A pretty bald blonde correctional officer approached me. "Aw, Jones, it'll be okay. What happened?"

"I got no bail. I gotta be in here until my court date, thirty days from now," I sobbed.

"I'm sorry, Here ..." She passed me a Kleenex.

"Pull yourself together before they see you crying." She signaled to the window full of faces watching my every move.

"Fuck these bitches," I replied angrily, snatching the tissue.

She was right, though. If I was to survive these next thirty days, I would have to man up, and fast. I dried my face, but it was still very evident I had been crying by the redness in my eyes. I entered the dorm, and the spectators noticed.

As I climbed on my bed, the dorm bully hissed, "Quit crying, you'll be here with me!" It brought zero comfort, but it wasn't meant to. I pulled the covers over my and silently cried until I fell asleep.

"Feelings come and go like clouds in a windy sky. Conscious breathing is my anchor."

- Thich Nhat Hanh -

8

Pranayama
THE PAUSE OF BREATH

"FEED UP!" I cringed at the sound every time they yelled it, calling us like animals. I hadn't really slept all night, but I was hungry so I was forced to get up. It was 5:30am the next day, and I had twenty-nine more days to go. This morning we were served 'shit on the shingles.' I wasn't sure who was given the task of naming the meals, but it was once again fitting. The mystery meat looked like dog food and oil. It was served with an apple, a carton of milk, and of course, three slices of bread. I asked for an alternate drink option but was shamed with laughter at the audacity to ask such a request.

Around noonish, I was called for an attorney visit. I was escorted down to the visitation room, where I met my new lawyer, Margaret Smead. She was a Jew who was known to devour the cases and with a $12,000 price tag, she'd better. She explained to me that the previous attorney was known to be a crook and expressed her sympathy for my case.

"I don't believe you would be so stupid to put your business in this, and nowhere in these charge papers do I see a reason for them to hold you. This is all about your husband. I will file for a second bail review, and we will get you out of here. It should take two to four weeks," she said with confidence. I felt good inside knowing I had a heavyweight champion in my corner.

Not even twenty minutes after I came back to the dorm did I witness what I thought was the craziest thing. The dorm had been on 'punishment' for about two weeks now, which meant nobody had been allowed to order commissary. Ultimately, there were probably only one to two people who were smart enough to stretch their last order far enough that they still had some. One of the two was an older lady probably in her late fifties. Her name was Samantha, but she went by Wheelz, I'm guessing because she pushed her wheelchair. Wheelz had multiple sclerosis, which means her bones were deteriorating. She kept herself active and mobile by using her wheelchair as a walker, and although she moved slowly with a slight limp, she had a friendly sense of humor, but she would crack slick if tested.

Dro and her gang decided they were hungry and didn't want to wait for dinner. When Wheelz went into her cubicle, Dro and her buddies approached her. "Bitch, run your tote." said Dro

Wheelz stood there with a *I ain't running shit* face, although she didn't say anything.

"You heard what the fuck I said?" another girl with Dro, named Jess spat as she made sure to step out of camera view.

Everyone knew that the cameras only really had a view of the dayroom. The cubicles, where we slept, and the back, by the showers, were out of view. Jess immediately rammed Wheelz, pushing her into her bed to hold her down and cover her mouth, while Dro grabbed for her tote of commissary. You could see that Wheelz was biting at Jess's hands but didn't have enough strength to push her off. Lily, a big and tall light-skin mama who was built similar to a female linebacker, came running like she was on a football field. With her arm out, she clipped Dro first, who dropped the tote in shock as she hit the ground. Dro wasn't going to give in that easy. After she realized what was happening, she picked up the tote as she rose from the ground and launched it at Lily, who was now pulling Jess from off of Wheelz. By this time, about six more girls jumped in. There was so much commotion going on that I wasn't sure who was fighting who. I sat straddled on my top bunk swinging my feet on both sides of the bed in total disbelief at what was happening. The entire dorm was watching this full-out brawl take place, crowding around the cubicle and standing on bunks to witness. Another minute went past; Lily had flipped someone over her back onto the ground and was now on top of her, pounding her face in. Jess jumped on her back, putting her into a headlock. Everyone was in such an uproar that they didn't notice the male guards bum-rushing through.

The six foot five, two hundred eighty-five pound male guard came in with a blue mask on his face, yelling, "TO YOUR BUNK ... NOW!"

This was followed by spraying the entire cube with a cloud-like substance. Immediately all fighting ceased because the fiery substance that was sprayed had everyone blind and burning. All guards ran out of the room and closed the bubble, locking us all in.

Damn, I can't believe he just pepper sprayed all of them, I said to myself, still sitting on my top bunk swinging my legs. It was all of five seconds later that the cloud made its way across the room and smacked me right in the face. I instantly lost my breath and joined the rest of the room in uncontrollable coughing. I coughed so much I began to gag. I went into a panic, unsure of what was really happening, and simultaneously fell off my top bunk. The hit to the concrete knocked the little bit of wind I did have right out of me. At first belly crawling, I slowly rose to my feet and watched my surroundings, I saw nothing but complete pandemonium. Everywhere the ladies were screaming and running for cover. I did the only thing that made sense to me at the moment and made my way to the back of the room. As I briskly walked, I saw terror in the eyes of the girls. Some were crying because their faces were burning, one even yelling, "My face is falling off!"

Many were pushing each other trying to get into the shower stalls in hopes the water would ease the pain. I stepped over two girls who were throwing up profusely from the coughing. In the last stall, there was one girl who had rounded up a carton of milk and was dumping it over her friend, who was currently in a fetal position on the molded shower floor. The carton she was pouring must have been from the day before because there were chunks of milk dropping on her eyes and mouth. The back of the room bought me all of thirteen seconds before I saw the gas creep its poison toward me. I realized I was in the farthest possible spot of the dorm, and the mist was about to consume me. I froze. I began to heave and felt the uncontrollable coughing setting in. My heart was racing, and I had complete fear that today would be my last day alive. The sheer horror I was witnessing slowed the room down for me, and once again, the silence set in. I could only hear the beat of my heart that I was sure was going to stop any second now. Time was up, the smoke was at my face, and I found myself on the ground.

My instincts must have kicked in because I was now coughing and crawling to a nearby bunk. As I threw up on myself, I grabbed someone's towel and dumped a cup of water onto it. Balling the towel up, I put the moist spot on my face. There was almost instant relief, and I could finally breathe again. I started taking deep breaths trying to regulate my heartbeat. I sat taking deep slow breaths in the corner, back against the wall, trying to keep calm in the chaos. Over the next forty minutes, I watched girls struggle to hold it together, some even running ass naked across the room because their skin was on fire.

Beginning to slowly count my breath, inhaling to four and then exhaling to four, I began to slow my heart rate. The more I concentrated on my breath, the more I could actually breathe and the more the noise around me began to subside. Thinking back to it, I believe I was "meditating," a practice where an individual uses a technique such as mindfulness or focusing the mind on a particular object, thought or activity to train attention and awareness and achieve a mentally clear and emotional calm and stable state.

When I returned to the room, my head was throbbing, but I heard a quiet that the dorm hadn't experienced before. The occasional cough and sniffle was all that came from the girls as most had crawled into their bunks to sleep the pain away.

"Can't say we ain't been through nothing together!" one inmate said.

I closed my eyes tight, trying to force myself to sleep. We had just survived my first fog!

OM: THE SELF WITHIN

*"You have to choose your path.
You have to determine what's worth fighting for.
You are the one who can determine your destiny"*

- NatalieAntoinette -

9

Saucha

PURE

Over the next couple of days, things seemed to be on repeat. Five-thirty breakfast, pretty much everyone went to sleep after, phones on at 9am, where only a few would actually get up.

Burn up the phone as much as I could until lunch at 10:30am, when the rest of the dorm got up, and then watch a fight, which happened faithfully. Wait for the phones to cut back on at 4:30pm while we ate dinner and waited for the next fight. We would be put on MSC for the rest of the night, and I would lie restless on my bunk. This went on for the next two weeks, and things definitely got old. Some fights included objects like brooms, cooler handles, or totes, but all were over in a matter of minutes. Sometimes a correctional officer would catch the culprit and sometimes not.

"Step to the back" were the initiating fighting words that signaled it was about to go down.

With a mix of ninety personalities, women who were pregnant, had mrsa, were detoxing from drugs, and some with mental health problems, the combination was a recipe for disaster. I remained as low key as possible and wanted to remain as active as I could. For the mornings, I would rise and do about twenty minutes of yoga every day. This was my stress relief on the outside, and I needed to find some sort of peace in this place.

There wasn't any equipment, so I used an extra blanket from someone who'd left as a mat on the floor. I did a series of pushups, squats, lunges, and crunched my pain away.

My birthday was only a few days away, and I wanted to start my twenty-ninth year on the most positive note possible, considering. My yoga routine was quickly noticed by onlookers, who first began with judgmental whispers. I can't say I didn't notice, but I carried on as if I didn't; it was the only option I had.

Commissary privileges were still revoked, and with dinner being served at 4:30pm and breakfast at 5:30am, tension was still pretty high. The only thing that kept time passing were the phones. A clip, the fifteen minutes your I.D. number provided for outgoing calls, was all that kept people sane. Unfortunately, once someone picked up on the receiving line, you would have to wait a whole forty-five minutes before you could go again. I think the intention was to make sure everyone could get a fair chance on the phone, but like everything else, there were loopholes. If you got in good with someone, they might let you use their clip, which meant you could 'double clip,' and some would even triple clip if they were bold enough. Phones ran from 9am to 2pm and again from 4:30pm to 10pm.

As the new kid on the block, I was informed on the rules. "In the morning, it's an open phone. There is a line to get in, and you use it as you please. The night phone is run by one person to each phone, there is a list. You'll be added to baby mama's phone." She signaled to the nine-month pregnant Black girl on the bottom bunk eating saltine crackers. "You will be called at night when it's your turn to go, and you just read this list and call the next person when you're done," she stated.

"Simple enough," I replied.

There were four phones, but only three worked, and about seventy-five women were split between each list. Needless to say, it was a battle to get second or third rounds at night. I made sure I was first in line just about every morning. This would ensure I got on the phone. I would pretty much grab my things I would need to discuss and sit by the phone around 8:45am. This was part of my routine, and pretty much the entire dorm knew it. All except Bonnie, who was a woman around the age of 52ish. She was 'stamped' in the streets as an 'OG,' or so I heard. She was dying of AIDS and was not afraid to express it, because she had little care for anything or anyone.

"I just don't give a fuck. I will kill you, your momma, and your kids, just so they don't grow up to be like you. Kill all you bitches!" she would yell at whoever for whatever.

She'd just gotten here about two days before and normally didn't get on the phone this early, but today was different. I had rounded my things up as usual and set everything up by the phone. I flipped the phone upside down to signal 'This phone is taken.' Where I messed up was I went to the bathroom, and by time I came out, Bonnie was standing at the phone I'd called.

"Bonnie, I flipped the phone, I'm first." I respectfully approached her.

"I don't give a fuck. I need to call my son. I'm getting on this phone."

"That's not how it works." It wasn't only me saying it, but a couple of the other early rising inmates chimed in.

If Bonnie went, then it wasn't just me getting rooted in the line. There were about four other people behind me, and none of them were happy. They all simultaneously barked at her, and her only response was, "Fuck y'all!"

She inhaled snot and spit from her throat and hocked it toward all of us. I was not only disgusted but appalled. In my mind, I wanted to leap at her for the amount of disrespect she'd just portrayed, but all I could think was, *I'm not fighting no chick with AIDS. I came in here clean. I will be damned if I get out with something! She wins.*

"Call me after you." I walked away, dodging a bullet.

> "Humility has to do with trying to be a vessel of purposes you're content to understand as not your own."
>
> - David Milch -

10

Buddhi

SHE WHO IS CONSCIOUS AND AWAKE

A FEW DAYS LATER, I was now 29. It was my birthday, and quite frankly, I was not feeling it. I woke up with a heavy heart but quickly tried to brush it away. I proceeded with the normal routine: brush my teeth, yoga, and food, but today I added prayer. Before I'd prayed all the time (mostly before meals, or to say thank you for waking the family up), but I realized it wasn't a part of my schedule. I wanted something to be different, but wasn't quite sure what. I just knew I needed change. I decided I would go on a fast, giving up food until Monday … it was Saturday.

It had been a few weeks since I had spoken to David, and he was on my heart that morning. Probably because I'd received my first kite from him the day before. A kite is a note sent from one prisoner to another. Usually a guard was cool enough to deliver it for you … if you were a lucky one. David had a cousin who worked here, making him one of the lucky ones. He expressed his apologies and admitted he was a changed man. He even gave me several Bible scriptures to reference (a first for him).

I was just elated to hear from him. The letter was even accompanied with a scent. I'm not sure if it really was the letter or my imagination conjured it up, but either way, I could smell him, and it made me miss him that much more today. All I really wanted, outside of my freedom of course, was to talk to David and our children. I just wanted them to wish me a *Happy Birthday*. Neither of those happened. There was a stabbing in the other dorm that morning over breakfast trays, so we were on MSC. Since that dream was destroyed, I tried to make the best of it. I was asked by several to host a yoga session. There were about twelve women who joined in the middle of the dayroom. The correctional officer told us to clear the room but decided to allow the activity once she saw what was happening. This lightened my spirit for the twenty-five minutes we practiced. It even made me smile a little because about eight of them requested we do it regularly. But once it was over, I had the birthday blues again.

I was approached by Tiffany. She looked creepy with a permanent smirk on her face and sharp green eyes, almost like a serial killer. She sat with me at the table and explained to me why she was here. She had been sentenced for false services. Tiffany was a psychic and had made hundreds of thousands from it, and I guess the state didn't like that. She furthermore said she'd picked up an energy from me and wanted to give me a reading. As a reiki practitioner, I believe very much in energy; however, I had my doubts about psychics. I hesitated a little but gave in because, well why not?

She began by telling me my case. That she saw the number four very strongly and that my husband was giving the number five. She didn't know what those numbers meant, but that's what she saw. She told me there seemed to be a generational curse on the women in my family, which honestly would explain a lot, and that I would be the one to break it.

Maybe that's why there are no patriarchal figures around, I thought to myself, but I gave no expression because I wanted to hear what she had to say. She rambled on a little more, and I thanked her for her time. Before I got up from the table, I couldn't help myself, I had to ask about my father. She closed her eyes, and it almost looked like she was reading inside her eyelids.

"Whoa." She opened her eyes and looked at me. "Your father has like a blue flame down his throat and chest." She signaled from her chin to her chest bone. "I've never seen anything like it," she continued. I sat now with a lump in my throat. My father was an alcoholic who had died when I was eleven from heart failure because he drank so much. "He seems to be stuck in the in-between." I shifted in my seat, now uncomfortably holding back tears.

"Is that why I can't see him in my dreams?" I found myself saying with a sound of desperate hope that I hadn't known I had.

"I keep seeing his hand going toward a woman's neck. Almost like he wants to choke her?" Her statement was almost a question. She didn't know that the alcohol had made my father abusive towards my mother. I silently shook my head, but this time streams were following.

"I see him going toward another woman too, maybe a sister." I acknowledged I knew the person. She was my stepmother, also abused by him.

"He's no longer stuck, and he says he's sorry and loves you. He wants to visit them first and will visit you after." I couldn't hold back this time. Today was not the day. I thanked her with a hug and went to the bathroom to get it together.

A few more fights broke out during the day. By the end of the night, as I sat calmly coloring a PJ Mask picture I drew to send to Michael and Michelle, guards came rushing in and fogged us. It was my worst birthday yet.

"She who is not content with what she has will not be content with what she wishes to have."

- NatalieAntoinette -

11

Santosha
CONTENTMENT

A FEW WEEKS LATER, it was approaching my court date. David had already gotten his second bail review, and his judge approved him for home detention. He would be released that night and sent home with the ankle monitor. He was my co-defendant, and we had the exact same charges, so I was sure to get approved on my bail review. My lawyer had put in for one a week back, so it would only be a matter of time. Good news was tomorrow was my scheduled court date, and this would all be behind me.

That morning when they called for court, I got up and dressed. I went to read my daily prayer, but no sooner had I opened my eyes than the correctional officer told me to get back to bed.

I had been indicted. I was devastated but not hopeless. I could go home on the box until my arraignment in December, another thirty days.

On Friday I received a letter from my lawyer. I had been denied my second bail review, which didn't even make sense. It stated they were going to enter another to a different judge. Hope was dwindling, but still present.

Saturday, we were fogged again.

Another week passed, and I received another letter. This time it was good news: I had been approved finally for my second bail review. I was confirmed by my lawyer that second bail reviews don't get approved to get denied. I would be going home come November 30th. Sadly, I would miss Thanksgiving but I'd live.

I had another week left. I made phone calls to ensure everyone was on the same page. The children were no longer being shuffled because their father was home, but our house, which was the 'crime scene,' was not allowed to be occupied by either defendant. Unfortunately, bills still had to be handled, so many conversations centered around that. My daughter, who I spoke with as often as I could, explained to me how she was going to make me a vanilla cake and throw me a surprise birthday party when I got home.

On the inside, I was dealing with a new bunkmate. She had just returned from the infirmary down Jessup because she'd had her baby five days before. She went by Money, and not long after she arrived did I realize why. Money and I were cool. We were both Scorpios and loved talking about our children—she had two boys. However, Money quickly became the dorm hustler. She had gotten a hold of some 'bukes' and was selling them for commissary at five dollars a pop. Your little piece would get you high for about eight hours or so, and all you had to give her was five dollars' worth of goodies, which could stretch pretty far. The entire dorm, or most of it anyway, were fiending for a quick escape. I remember looking around and noticing how zombied out and sluggish the dorm was moving at one point, kind of like a small scene from The Walking Dead. It was quite comical, come to think of it, and yet also very sad on a much deeper level.

On Wednesday, commissary day, Money had three totes full of items, and detainees were lining up one by one to pay off their debts. We were allowed to order fifty dollars' worth of items per week, and one girl had to pay forty-five dollars' worth. She was getting high pretty much every day. She came with a tote full and left with only her coffee and creamer. That seemed to be okay with her, though. The White girls loved their coffee! Not to mention all the perks I got for being the plug's roommate. Everyone was happy, and I was fed.

Okay, so little disclaimer. I am not proud of all the actions I took during this journey. Hold your judgment because we haven't even gotten to the good part. This was a journey that I clearly needed to embark on.

In addition, it was the birthday of one of the inmates. This was our first commissary, since I'd gotten there at least, and for the first time everyone was happy, as much as you could be in jail anyway. To celebrate, we decided to throw a birthday bash for our friend Coco. Coco was a thirty-one-year-old sweetie pie who was addicted to narcotics. As a result she had no front teeth. She was cool with everyone, so it made it easy to bring everyone together for a good time. Strawberry, who we called Berry, and who was also dating Coco at the time, was known to be really creative and an amazing chef. She smashed a bunch of deluxe cookies and wafers, pressing it together to make a small layer of cake. Tootsie rolls, fireballs, butterscotch, and lemon drops were in rotation, and everyone had oatmeal creme pies or Swiss rolls of their own. Angel, an old detainee known for putting a mean finger roll in your head, was using tampon holders to curl Wheelz' hair. The tampon curlers were held into place by the rim of a ripped glove. We grabbed a couple sheets from the beds of volunteers and tied them together, making one long sheet.

First it was tug of war. About eight girls went to battle until eventually the sheet tore and all hit the ground in pure laughter. Next they jumped rope, taking turns jumping in and out until finally they gathered more sheets to double dutch. Feeling the positive energy, even I had to join in on the double dutch. It felt good to let my little kid out, even if for a couple of minutes. With everyone either jacked up on sugar or high from "the three," we seemed to be okay.

Two inmates volunteered to take it up a notch. In one cubicle, about three girls were at work making cigarettes. Cigarettes were made with a tampon wrapper (because nothing went to waste around here). It was carefully opened like a paper for a joint, laced with muscle rub for a menthol effect and the contents of a tea bag because you could get forty bags for a dollar and forty-seven cents off commissary. I later tried one hit of it out of curiosity, and to my surprise, it was very much like a cigarette... disgusting! In the next cubicle, Lily had now ripped up a sheet and was making very skimpy outfits for Diamond and Crystal, who had both been strippers or prostitutes at some point. The sheet acted as lingerie and wrapped around the neck, under the boobs, and cupped the booty. I was quite impressed. Once ready, Troy dropped a beat, and the show commenced. Everyone huddled around as Diamond and Crystal twerked and ass-clapped all over the place. Diamond got on Coco and started grinding while Crystal was lying on the floor, legs straight in the air, making her butt wiggle. The spectators oohed and ahhed, and some threw fake money that had been made previously from all the unused grievance forms. The paper was green, so it made a realistic effect. The night ended with a little karaoke. The majority of the dorm was having a blast thinking of oldies but goodies to sing along to. Slowly but surely, the sugar rush died down, and singers began to taper off as we crawled into bed, not wanting the fun to end but accepting the reality that we were tired. I fell asleep singing Frank Ocean "Thinking about You" with a smile on my face. Finally, a good day!

It was time for my second bail review, and I was more than ready to return home. Like a kid at Christmas, I couldn't sleep the night before, excited with anticipation. I wanted Chipotle and a glass of wine so bad, I could almost taste it. Around 9 o' clock I was escorted to the third floor. I was expecting to leave the building this time, but I guess it was nice to see a different part of the building too. I entered a row with four rows of four chairs and went to the front. Eventually three male inmates came in and sat in the rows behind me. I had zero interest in turning around. I just wanted the judge to hurry up so I could go hug and steal kisses from my babies. My heart ached for them daily.

The judge entered. *Yes, a Black lady*, I thought.

My case was first. The state attorney stood up and began to read my charges. My eyes grew wide as she read an additional six charges that, unbeknownst to me, had been added. I watched the judge's unenthused face begin to calculate the pounds of CDS the attorney was throwing out. I'm almost certain she was reading the same charges twice because the list seemed never-ending. I didn't recall that much contraband, but I was also beginning to get nauseous. I sounded like a terrible human, according to this prosecutor. When was someone going to ask me a question or let me explain? Thank God it was now my lawyers turn. Margaret approached the bench.

"Your honor. Mrs. Jones is a hard-working woman. She poses no threat to the community as she has much support from them. We have some here today." She was referring to my mother, mother-in-law, and three friends from high school: Irene, Sombo, and Saba, who were like my sisters. "She has two children who are in need of her care, your honor," she continued. "Furthermore, her co-defendant is currently out on home detention."

As the judge shifted in her seat, my gut began to twist. Yet again, this didn't feel right. The judge interrupted. "That's nice." Sarcasm was all over her response. "Most indicted cases are not being seen until March and April." She sounded a little more empathetic that time. It didn't last long. "But I would be a fool to consider home monitoring because how could I be sure it would stop the empire Mrs. Jones is running?"

My lawyer started to open her mouth but was quickly silenced.

"Mrs. Jones knows what she's doing, and quite frankly, appears to be a queen pin. ... DENIED!!"

I closed my eyes and let out a breath, stunned. I could hear the confusion and fuss from my mother in the distance on the monitor, and my heart was all the way in my toes at this point. The officer came and dragged me out, and it wasn't until I was pulled out of the room I noticed I wasn't breathing.

Did she say March? Does she know it's November? What about my children? I will not make it. Did she even see me through the monitor? Maybe if I just spoke up? ... So many thoughts ran through my head. MARCH!!! I could barely feel my legs. A lady officer escorted me back to what would be my new home for the next five months, slowly and gently. I don't know if she heard or my expression caused the gesture, but her understanding was much appreciated. It was probably my tenth step that I couldn't feel anything. I began to hyperventilate, and my eyes welled up with so much water I could no longer see. I collapsed onto the floor in search of my breath, crying hysterically. I had just been beheaded. Or at least I felt like it.

"I'm truly innocent and now I have to miss ..." That was all I could get out. "Why, God?"

She helped me from the floor. "You have to keep walking," she whispered as though we would be killed if caught otherwise. Doing my best, we fractionally crawled back to five south. Once we made it to the elevator, she turned to me. "Do you believe in God?"

Not anymore was my first thought. I reluctantly shook my head yes, not able to look into her face.

"Do not give up your faith. Lean on God, he will pull you through. Keep your faith." The elevator doors opened. When I saw the dorm again I lost it. It was uncontrollable. Luckily everyone was asleep, and the phones were open. Still sobbing, I called David on his cell.

"Baby, I'm so sorry," is how he greeted me. I could hear the pain in his voice.

I cried so hard I woke a couple inmates up. "March ..." is all I could say. I was sick.

"I've been advised to do something." David's voice was cracking through the phone. He was referring to confessing everything. The idea was that he would take the heat, and I would be immediately released.

With only our children on my mind, I protested, "If you come clean now, they are only going to put you in here. Then our children will not have either of us until this is over. Let's see all the other options first and that be the last thing. I will never forgive you if you abandon our children." I didn't really want to say those words, but my thought process wouldn't allow him to turn himself back in. No point in us both being here. I broke down maybe two more times on the phone, then gave up. We made a plan, said our goodbyes, and I hung up.

The game plan: submit for a private box to allow me to go home. As I had only been denied by the state issued box, there was still hope to see the outside before our court date in March. If all else failed, then he would turn himself in to get me released. I would stick it out for a few more weeks if it meant we both went free. If not, he would sacrifice for the sake of my freedom. That's what you do as a team. That's how you hold each other down. Right?

I crawled back into bed and was once again sobbing my way to sleep with the new realization that I had to make this "home" a little while longer.

12

Pratyahara
WITHDRAWAL OF SENSES

"FEEEED UPP YAWWWWW!" Ugh, I had daysssss more of this nonsense. My eyes were close to being swollen shut from all the tears that met my drenched pillow. It was dinner time again and we were having 'pepper steak,' which turned out to be a super dried piece of hamburger served with three slices of bread and more fruit medley. As I played around in my food, I noticed something squirming in my fruit. It was a maggot, two of them actually. I was absolutely disgusted and went to tell the guard.

"Just throw it away, nothing I can do about it" was the response, which seemed to be the response for pretty much every problem. Nobody actually cared enough to do anything. She wouldn't give me another tray either. You either Eat it or Leave it! I was over how unethical this whole situation was.

※

Someone had secretly put in a private home detention application for me, and it turned out to be a big-time political face of Baltimore who just so happened to have a massive crush on David. Why she chose to help me (or so I thought) I can't be sure, but I was ever grateful. I had been approved and given a pick-up date of January 6, 2019. It was after the holidays and New Years, yes, but it was before my court date and most importantly, the same day as my daughter's birthday. I was going to be home at least for my baby girl's fourth birthday. I was elated, once again counting down the sleeps.

Weeks passed, and every day I counted. Twenty-seven days, to be exact. I had 13 days left when my world was once again.... crushed! My family finally told me that they'd taken back my acceptance almost two weeks before, but nobody wanted to tell me because it was going to crush my spirit. They were right: I was devastated, and at this point, I lost all hope. I didn't know if I was more hurt that I wasn't going home or that nobody told me I was building up false hope.

That was my last straw; there were no more cards to play.

I felt helpless in so many ways. As I sat on my bunk dreaming of better days, my bunkmate interrupted my thoughts.

"Newnew, you wanna try some?" Money was once again offering me a buke. She had done so the days before but was not at all shocked when I turned it down each time. The look on her face when I said "Why the hell not" was priceless. She thought I was joking until I sat up with a *Girl, I'm not playing* look on my face.

"Awwwww shit," she laughed to herself, cutting me a small share from the strip. "You have three options: you can put it in your eye, toot it, or put it in your butt. I like putting it in my butt."

Chuckling at the fact that I was too far to go back now, I selected the butt option. After watching so many go through the burning sensation of the eye, I was not for it, and putting something up my nose didn't seem appealing either. She gave me a glove and walked with me to the bathroom. She instructed me from the next stall, "Put it on your pointer and wet it with just a drop of water. Stick your finger halfway up and swish it around."

I definitely couldn't go back now. I shook my head.

"Leave it for thirty seconds and then check your finger to make sure it's all gone." She finished up and left. "I'll be back."

I was left in the bathroom with my finger up my ass, wondering what would happen next—not a good look.

When does it kick in? What will I feel? I was full of questions and anticipation. It was about forty-five minutes later and I felt nothing.

"I feel mine. You should feel it by now." She was breaking an even smaller piece now. "Try this."

Wanting to feel something so bad and find an escape from here, I took the piece and decided to take a more direct approach. Still not ready for the eye burn, I placed the orange piece onto a spoon and watched as they added a dime of water to it, mixed it for a second. The piece was now a solution I put into my nose and let it run down my throat. It took all of ten minutes before I think both pieces hit me because I was in a whole other world. My eyes went low and the room slowed. I felt GOOD! I lay in my bed listening to stripper stories, drug deals gone bad, and murder mysteries but felt no connection. It was like I was there but not there at all. I think this is considered an out of body experience.

Just as I closed my eyes to enjoy the ride, they popped open wide. I was about to upchuck, and it was coming fast. Rushing to the bathroom, I just got the little bit of food I had eaten into the toilet. That was the first of about five that night. Apparently, these are the side effects of your first trip. Even the water I would sip came right back up. I was a little frustrated because I actually was hungry, but any thought of consuming something was long lost. Probably two hours later, I was able to calm down enough that I could lie still. Floating on cloud nine, I drifted peacefully into a nice and much-needed rest.

The next dinner I was convinced to try again. Hesitant because I was not much in the mood for vomiting but remembering how the floating sensation was quite enticing, I tooted another piece. I was once again on a cloud, but this time I enjoyed the entire ride. Throwing up all your leftovers is only the result of virgin stomachs, and I guess I was now seasoned. I found myself drifting in my sentence. My eyes would shut slowly, and when I finally noticed to blink them open again, I found myself in a lean. I think they called this nodding. It heightened the experience, but I could only imagine I looked like the typical crackhead at the bus stop who would be bent all the way over but never hit the ground. For this brief moment, I was not pressured with the downs of life. As I fell asleep that night, I made a vow not to do these drugs again. I enjoyed it too much and saw a drug addiction alert flash before my eyes. I completely understand how people get hooked. It gives a brief moment of peace and takes you away from all the stress you're feeling. But it's only for the moment.

"Be not the ways of the world." I think that was the first time I heard God.

The next day started pretty normally. There were a few verbal arguments, but everyone managed to dodge a real fight, which was a blessing. I was quite tired of the fussing and being on lock down. I really wanted another play day, not because I wanted my little kid free but because I really just wanted some peace and unity. It was lunchtime, and my favorite meal was being served. Taco Tuesday. The serving was the size of a kid's happy meal, and the meat was still unidentifiable, but it had a little flavor so I wasn't going to complain. I struggled to get the first tray down normally so I would never find myself in the second tray line. Inmates were already lining up, so I had to leave my stuff at the table to get back in line. There were usually only six to nine extra trays, so it was now or never. As I waited for my tray, I found my mouth watering because I would finally eat something that wasn't too hard to get down. Taco Tuesday only came once a month, if that. I counted out, and I was to get the last tray. There were three people in front of me and four trays. At the very last minute, someone came over and rooted the person in front of me. I didn't get a tray, but I didn't feel like a fight either. To my surprise, I found my tray still in place when I returned. Any other time the whole thing would be missing, especially when you had nobody watching your back, but I must have gotten lucky. I devoured my two half-full hard tacos and went to wash it down with my water.

They serve every meal with a flavored base, which I found out is actually pipe cleaner that comes in a 'not for human consumption' plastic bag. I'm not honestly sure how they get away with so many illegal and inhumane actions, but this is a true story.

Needless to say, when I found that out, I stopped drinking it and only consumed the toilet water that I tried to convince myself was better.

I was so thirsty I took the water straight back, not even tasting it until I was half done with the cup. Something wasn't right. I smelled the cup. It was tinted yellow with bubbles in it. It smelled of pure bleach. My throat started to tingle and felt dry, while my chest burned, and my stomach flipped. Someone had poured bleach in my cup.

> *"They say the closer you get to God, the harder the devil works to tear you down. Stay focused!"*
>
> *- NatalieAntoinette -*

My body ran hot as a fever spiked, and I spent the rest of time running back and forth, throwing up. I tried calling for the nurse, but they said that I needed to put in a sick call and wait, which took three to four days. When I wasn't puking, I lay in my bed for rest, mad at myself for slipping and at God for letting humanity come to this. I didn't deserve any of this.

Okay, so maybe I stole watermelon bubble gum a few times, because who doesn't like watermelon Bubblicious? Maybe I skipped out on a bill or two, because I was a stupid high school kid who couldn't really afford a $15 meal, or even lied to my mom about where I really was after school, although some could argue about whether that is actually being bad. Did any of that land me in the luxury apartments of Central Bookings with real murderers?

I was burning up in my bed but shaking from the cold, when I heard the whispers and "fuck yous" beginning to stir up. Not wanting to, I peeked my head from the covers. Vee, who was a twenty-one-year-old girl who was on testerone pills and now looked and sounded like a man, was squared up with Denny, a forty-five year old Dom with dreads in the back of the dorm. I will say this was the quietest fight of the dorm; however, what I saw next still haunts me. Denny seemed to have something in her hand, but Vee moved so fast, the object was no match. Vee came with a powerful three piece, knocking the dentures in Denny's mouth straight through her cheek. Vee grabbed the item from her hand, which turned out to be a disassembled pen with a razor blade attached, and swung, slashing right down Denny's face leaving an open gash from the left corner eyebrow to the left nostril.

Denny was left in a puddle of blood on the floor as Vee spit on her and walked calmly away. I guess it was the fact that everyone stood with their hands over their mouths that raised suspicion and caused the guard, who had been too occupied by the other male guard visiting our floor to notice. When she came in and finally made her way to the back, you could hear her screech and call for backup. Another female rushed in, and as they dragged Denny out, the army of male correctional officers came in. Without question, we were once again fogged. It was another scurry for safety, but this time I was battling the fever as well. It was the hardest fog yet, but forty-five minutes later, we were all still alive. The dorm had an eerie silence about it, and someone decided to cut on the news.

After not even five minutes of news, two inmates who were actually blood sisters started screaming. It was hard to make out at first, but once you could hear them clearer, they were saying, "NO,NO,NO,NOT MY BABY!!" from one.

"OMG THAT'S MY NIECE," the other was screaming hysterically. Apparently her only surviving child—the other child had been shot and killed only five months ago—had just been shot in a drive-by and in unknown conditions. A beautiful picture of a five-year-old smiling child was now plastered on the TV. The entire spirit of the dorm dropped. Some started praying, some crying, others just walking around confused, lost or hurt, but nobody knew what to say, not even me. The majority of the women in here were mothers, so we all felt the pain. I went into shock because that could have been anybody, and there was nothing anyone could do about it. The dorm remained silent the rest of the night. All I could do was pray.

After a restless night of tossing and turning, I woke up with a case of the shakes, bad. My legs and hands resembled someone with tremors, and my mind was on 1000 percent. All I wanted to do was talk to my babies, but I couldn't because we were still on MSC. I felt like I had absolutely no control over anything. Not my marriage, children, business...

not my life. For the first time in a long time, I was helpless and had no way to correct it. My shaking became uncontrollable, and I started crying. The correctional officers pulled me to the side and called down for mental health. I was having a nervous breakdown.

"When you choose an action, you also choose the consequence of that action. In anything you do, Let Love Lead"

- NatalieAntoinette -

13

Ahimsa
NON HARMING

AFTER ABOUT AN hour of discussion with the psych doctor, she told me I wasn't a normal case to come in, and she didn't think I would need meds long term but prescribed me a medium dosage of Zoloft, an antidepressant. She said it appeared I was suffering from Bipolar Depression. I was prescribed this once after my second birth for postpartum but refused the meds because I felt ashamed that it seemed I needed those. It didn't help that David said I was weak for needing it and threatened that he wouldn't want to be with someone stuck on drugs… oh the irony!

I wasn't feeling like myself lately and could admit that. Only crying in the privacy of my shower, my problems were not public and shouldn't be shown, so I covered it with smiles. *Maybe there was a reason I am faced with the same challenge again*, I thought to myself. I signed the acceptance form and walked away, feeling half guilty and half accomplished.

I had gotten in good with one of the C.O.s when I got back. I asked if she could sneak me a few pieces of paper and something to write with. It took her what seemed like hours, but she returned with about six sheets and a pen so I could start journaling.

I began writing until my hand hurt. I wrote about what I felt, how we were treated, and my desires and fears. I wrote about anything that came to mind until I had nothing left to write. I had emptied my mind on the sheet, and now I was clear. I had room to think straight and problem solve. These pages became my safe pages, a space to release my mind and clear my heart. I took to journaling every day. Even if I only filled one page, I created the time to write, which I clearly had the space to do.

⚜

Trying to take my mind off my reality, I did what I knew I had to. There were too many families at stake who depended on the income of the business. I began to focus my mind back on the business and the fact that there was still an 'empire' that needed to be run. After working out a schedule that would allow the children to be properly cared for with little disruption to the lives of the caretakers, I had to put on my big girl panties. I couldn't spend the remainder of the time crying with confusion over the unchangeable. Time came to delegate the tasks appropriately. Festivals and shows were already paid for, the second location was open, and the airport had to remain upright. There was work to be done, so phone calls began to become business centered. My assistant and mother answered every time I called. We only had fifteen minutes, so I would include as much detail as possible. I gave email access, contacts, and inventory management instructions. I wanted to use my time wisely, and it was already 8pm. I was fourteenth on the list, but everyone in front of me seemed to want to double clip. Now my turn, I grabbed my pen and paper, which was the back of a crossword puzzle, and rushed to the phone. I called Ma Dukes, who conferenced in Donna. As fast as I could, I ran through the importance of their help, procedures for reporting airport documents, how to follow up with the health department for the new location, ways to increase revenue and decrease labor, and began to create a list of who would handle which task by such date. It wasn't long before the operator butted in. "You have 60 seconds remaining."

Unfortunately, we weren't done. I needed maybe five to ten more minutes, but fortunately, one of my bunkmates was done for the night and was willing to let me use her clip. I called Tonya over, who entered in her information and went about her way. As I sat back down on the tote being used as a chair, Keya, who resembled a brown-skin version of Quagmire from Family Guy, the girl who was next on the phone, approached me.

"It's my turn," she said, looking down on me.

"I know, but everyone else took so long. I'm not going to get another round." I looked up with an apology in my voice. She must have picked up on it and took it as an invite to take it further.

"I don't give a fuck, it's my turn," she spat coldly. Annoyed at her rudeness, I heard the phone beginning to ring.

"Okay, I'll only be like five minutes, I swear. It's really important. I gotta ..." *Click* ... She had hung up my clip.

"I'm not a fucking psychiatrist, it's my fucking go. Move, bitch!" She stood still, hovering right over my head. At this point I was looking down at her shoes, which were all of eight inches away from mine. The dorm had gotten quiet, and I could feel the eyes piercing through my clothes.

Now, after a year of boxing and loads of anger management classes, I had learned how to walk away from my troubled past, and words don't really affect me the way they once did. Calling me a 'bitch' just didn't trigger me anymore. I was more of a principle's girl, and right now, whether she actually wasted my clip or not didn't matter to me. Right now, the principle was that she had disrespectfully hung up my clip, and as much respect as I gave around here trying to keep peace, I did not approve.

My body got a wave of heat, and I began to grip the phone in both my hands, trying to decide what move I was going to make next. Fight now so I didn't have to fight again, or be the bigger person, jeopardizing my safety the rest of this stay? Twisting the phone in my hands, I seriously contemplated breaking the entire shit, wringing the girl's neck out, and walking away. I didn't want any trouble, but I really needed to place this call; tomorrow was a deadline we couldn't afford to miss. Nonetheless, I called on my inner maturity to walk away and decided I would hang up the phone. Then she blurted, "Right! ...Bitch" and went to spit.

I'm not sure why this is the thing to do around here, but this time her smelly spit landed straight on my shirt and a little bit even on my cheek. I dug my heel into the ground and put all my leg power to work as I leaped to my feet, my fist involuntarily following. Before I was balanced on my legs, I had uppercut Keya. I think she was as shocked as the rest of the dorm because she took a second before she went to ball her fist for a return strike. It was just long enough for me to get into my stance, left foot forward, right arm leading, I was ready to block her blow. A crowd was now forming trying to pull us apart because truth was, if we fought, NOBODY was using the phone tonight. She quickly threw a punch which my face dodged but my shoulder caught. Right as my bunkmate grabbed to yank me, I gave a swift left to her jaw, barely connecting but striking enough to count as a hit.

"Don't ever disrespect me when I'm talking to my mother ... Bitch!" I was mad. The correctional officer was watching the whole time, and as I was walking back to my bunk, she gave me a wink.

The phones were cut off, of course, but she'd winked, so I just knew everything would be all right. About ten minutes passed, and there was still a bunch of chatter roaming the dorm. The correctional officer came in.

"Jones ... pack up!" It got quiet.

I was going on lock.

OM: THE SELF WITHIN

"You can either be a host to God, or a hostage to your ego. The choice is yours to make. Choose wisely"

- NatalieAntoinette -

14

Brahmacharya
A WALK WITH GOD

I WAS BEING SHIPPED to four center. It was only a floor down, but the set-up was a little different. The ten metal tables still sat in the center of the room, and there were six showers in the back, but the difference was in the sleeping arrangements. To each side was about ten cells. Each cell had one metal bunk bed and a toilet with an attached sink. The doors were solid metal and there was a small peephole window to see into the dayroom. I was now on twenty-three and one, meaning I was on lock for twenty-three hours and got to come out of the cell for one hour, in which I would need to get accomplished whatever I saw fit. The only real options were the phones and a shower. Everyone was let out at the same time, so the battle for the phone was even tougher. I didn't even bother. I was too strained, and quite frankly didn't feel like the fuss. Not to mention all my recent phone calls were about family problems. Thelma was sick of looking at David, David felt ashamed and hopeless, the children were causing problems with scheduling, the business was doing horrible in sales, which I found out from my accountant because my mother wouldn't tell me, the house needed to be sold, the list was unending. Even behind bars I was expected to come up with solutions. I needed to remain the strong one, and right now, I wasn't feeling so strong. I was feeling really low and had no one to get it off my chest to. I felt alone. Not to mention, the last conversation I had with David didn't sit well with me. Since David and

I were co-defendants, I was technically not supposed to converse with him. Anytime we did chat was through another inmate's line, and it was brief, mostly chatting with the children.

One night, I had a dream, and I had to wonder about its meaning. Like our daughter, whenever I had a dream I remembered, it was a sign of something. This dream caused me to call David and ask if he'd ever cheated. It was random and caught him totally off guard, but he chose to be honest and admitted it. He had committed this crime prior to the lock up and was going to tell me when I came home, or so he said. I wasn't in the least bit shocked, just disappointed. I wasn't fulfilling my duties as a wife, so what would I expect? But it didn't stop me from feeling like a fool or the pain that hit my chest for once again being right about some painful news. David then told me that he thought it was best to wait until I got home to discuss. In the short amount of time he was in jail, he witnessed a lot of men arguing on the phone with their significant others. He wanted to refrain from that, which is understandable, but also it pissed me off on a whole other level. I was his wife, and if there was anyone I would want to talk to, it would be him.

Keep in mind, we are more than 10 years into this relationship, so as much as I was upset, I was not at all surprised.

What did shock me was the conversation that followed. I confronted him about the plea offered to me from the jump. I told him that if I'd snitched I could have been out.

I guess I was looking for a pat on the back or something because when his response came in as "Well, you should have taken the deal, because I'm going to trial," my stomach fell to my butt. I couldn't believe my ears. If you recall, the agreement was, we do everything to try to get me out first, and as a last straw, he takes the plea. Now it was time to 'pull the trigger,' and the deal was out the window. I didn't know if it was the pill I was taking or if he really was tripping. I was lost, hurt, and confused all in one. I couldn't believe my ears. Needless to say, it had me feeling like a team player for a team of one. So, secretly, I looked forward to time in my cell. It was a chance to hear myself think, or else I would have gone crazy. I didn't know what was about to happen, but I would soon find out.

The one perk I did instantly find in my new four corners was a light switch. I flicked it off and tried to force myself to sleep.

"FEED UP!" The greeting was no different. There was a loud bang on the door, the mail slot opened, and a tray was slid into it. This happened for all three meals. We came out from 7pm-8pm, in which I briefly caught up with any familiar face in the room. I took a cold shower and headed straight back to my bunk. All of the 'troublemakers' were now down here, so of course this little hour led to a fight. I just sat in my cell, door open, waiting to be closed back in. I was lucky enough not to have a roommate at the moment, so I was really faced with myself. Once officially locked back in, I found myself crying. This time, not because I knew I had so many months, but because all of my fears, the ones I had been running from pretty much my whole life, I now had to face. It was sad and ironic all in one.

For so long, I had been fighting postpartum depression. I'd always wanted my children to grow up in a two-parent household, and I never wanted a divorce, yet I was facing all of the above. I have always found a way to control a situation, never wanting to become a victim of my circumstances, but I had absolutely no control over anything in my life right now. There were so many problems I was facing, and I was losing my mind because I had no answers. I felt helpless, and as thoughts ran through my head and my sobbing began to slow, I began to focus on my breath. I felt something shift in me. It seemed like every fear was gathering like storm clouds in my mind.

I met God here. I would lie there praying and praying for a sign or some understanding. I would ask for a miracle and make promises that I genuinely meant but my human flesh probably wouldn't allow me to keep.

I prayed for peace over the family, as worldly things were causing confusion and strife.

I prayed for understanding spirits. So many lost souls need guidance

I prayed for compassion, that we would begin to love another as we love ourselves.

I prayed that we would begin to love ourselves.

Help us to love ourselves!

I asked for complete forgiveness and for help in forgiving myself.

I prayed for clarity!

I released all bondages and gave all weight to God. It took this very moment to realize I cannot control outcomes. God is responsible. He will make a way from no way. He had led me through everything else. I had to let go of the guilt, the shame, the judgment, fear, doubt, insecurities, anger, and any other indifference I had. I had to remove myself from the battles that were not mine to fight. I had to accept the wounds left from previous battles and realize the marks are signs of strength on a true soldier, not weaknesses.

"Be still, daughter, be still and know that I am God, a strong tower, a refuge for you!"

The words seemed to breathe peace into me, calm my soul, and give me a strangely curious hope. Something was happening with me. Something that led me back to my faith. I remained in darkness the majority of my days. I ate because I had to and showered every other day. I had officially been beheaded.

I guess the correctional officer put in a good word for me because I was only on lock for four days. It felt like forever, but turned out it wasn't that long. They brought me back up to the general population on A dorm. New faces and new rules, which meant more excitement around the corner. * insert eye rolling emoji*

"The most important person you will ever meet in life is your higher self. So it is imperative to stay connected to our inner self, as it is the very essence of who we are."

- NatalieAntoinette -

15

OM
THE SELF WITHIN

*T*HEY SAY THE closer you get to God, the more the devil tries to intervene. I was starting to believe that was true based off the next set of events that took place.

My first couple of days back were kind of quiet. Word had already made it around the dorm of why I went to and from lock. I wasn't bothered much, which I didn't mind. Not until today. It all started with a kite. I'm not sure how it got there, but when I came back from the bathroom, there was a folded piece of paper on my pillow with a lot of hearts. It read:

"Newnew I love the way you carry yourself. I have been watching you since day one and I'm glad you're finally on this side. I want to know what you taste like. I know you may not be into girls or whatever but it's something about that walk. If you ever decide to switch over, I want to be the one. I'll be waiting. - your secret admirer"

I dropped the note wide-eyed and slightly blushing. I gazed around the room, hoping to catch eyes with someone to reveal who wrote the note, but it didn't seem anyone was paying attention to me.

Days later, as I was washing my face in the shower, I heard movement behind me. Oftentimes someone would stick their bowl or cup in the shower to get some luke warm water. This was how we made coffee or noodles. Without looking I said, "What do you need?"

"Newnew, do you have any more Motrin?" I heard a voice that was closer than expected.

She was referring to the cup of pills I had hidden under my mattress. Since day five I'd had headaches pretty much every day. Call it the stress, or maybe it was from all the mold in the place, or maybe a combination of both. I'm not sure what the real reason was; I just know that I was prescribed 800 mg of Motrin, and they wanted me to take it three times a day, literally every day. *Talk about drug OD*. Hence the stack of unused pills that was now used as commissary money.

Quickly rinsing my face, I turned to find Nip, a dark-skin bug-eyed little thing standing naked in a towel behind me.

"GIRL, WTF is you doing?" She was standing there with a devilish grin.

"Nip, get the hell out my shower before I whoop your ass." I was a little nervous but was already prepared to pluck her if needed.

"I really just wanted to see your body and it's a *nice* body." She licked her lips and looked at me from head to toe.

"Let me get a Motrin when you get out." She slid out of the shower, watching me until she was gone. I released a breath I didn't know I was holding. I retreated to my bunk, ready to call it a night when I heard some chuckles from the cubicle next to me. Peeking over the wall, I saw them making something. There was a mini class going on, and Berry was the teacher. She had a few wet tampons, pads, and tissue that she was rolling up in the cellophane from our lunch sandwiches. She then shoved it down the finger of a glove and began molding it. Before you knew it, she was holding what looked like a dildo.

"Viola, there you have a SD."

I couldn't help but butt in. "What's an SD?" I was intrigued by how creative you can be in jail.

"A State Dick!" the girls chuckled. I shook my head and lay back down. At some point, I dozed off because I was dreaming that there was a subtle kiss to my lips. I felt the pressure on my lips again, but this time I felt teeth. Then I realized I wasn't dreaming at all. I opened my eyes to Nip biting my lip ever so sweetly. Without hesitation *whoop*—I had smacked her across the face.

"The hell is wrong with you, man?" I was wiping my mouth, pissed.

"I'm sorry, baby. I thought you'd like that."

"Back the fuck up before I bang you, yo. I'm not even fucking play'in."

She was now climbing off the side table that she had been standing on to reach me.

"My bad, you got it." She backed away. I watched her until she was out of sight.

Then I got a glance of some commotion across the dorm. Directly across from me was Dre and her friend leaving Anna's cubicle. Anna was a small little spanish chic who could not speak English and had a very innocent demeanor.

Dre had the SD in her hand and was high-fiving her friend. Anna lay on her bed, holding her blanket and silently crying. Too angry to care, I rolled over and eventually went back to sleep.

After lunch the next day, there was a sign-up list for up to fifteen inmates who wanted to go to a church service. I really wanted to just catch a breath of fresh air and honestly could use a prayer or two, so I made sure to sign up. One of my bunkmates, Dora, signed up behind me. When it was time to line up, I excitedly ran to the line. It had been months since I'd been outside. Dora had decided she was no longer coming. I saw a glazed look in her eye that made me question her.

"Are you high, Dora?"

She laughed and said no, but I knew she was lying. I was too invested to plead with her, and it was time. I gave my grievance with my eyes, which I could tell she recognized, and departed. To my disappointment, the church was through a door in a back room.

It was a different set of four walls, so I accepted. Positive thinking here!

In service, coincidently.... or not... we talked about forgiveness. There were two Black ladies as guest speakers who gave testimony of how they were once prisoners themselves. They spoke on how Jesus had to forgive, even those who directly betrayed him. They had us close our eyes and think of all those who might have hurt us, abandoned us, touched us, or pained us in any way.

As my eyes were closed I felt a tug in my heart, and so many people flashed before my eyes. I didn't even know I felt this way, but the one that stuck out the most was myself. I was a victim to my own story because I was not willing to accept, forgive, and let go of my past. I had brushed so many things under the rug and wanted to hide from and ignore the very things that made me strong.

What exactly did I need to forgive myself for? Well, that's a whole other book my dear. But know that the chapters run deep!

It was time to forgive myself and let it all go. And I was ready. A tear welled up in my closed eye and made its way down my cold cheek. I felt relief, as if there were chains attached to my wrist that were finally broken. I had been hiding behind my nickname, Newnew, for so long, running from my past. Suddenly, I appreciated Natalie, my true self. I forgave me!

Church ended, and on the way out, I picked up a book, Sixty Days of Prayer. There was no better time to start than now.

When we got back to the dorm, a lot of commotion was taking place. Dre was being escorted out of the room. She was heading downstairs to get rebooked for a PREA (Prevent Rape Elimination Act) violation. She was getting a rape charge for last night's activity with Anna. *Poor Anna!*

Simultaneously, there was a music video taking place in a cubicle a couple doors down. Inmates were banging on totes and walls to club mix beat and at the center of the commotion was Dora.

Dora had recently gained a lot of weight, and most of it was in her newfound Spanish booty. Needless to say, this was all the ammo she needed to show everyone her new twerking abilities. About ten minutes into the hooting and hollering, Dora began gyrating so hard her eyes began to roll back into her head. All movement stopped, and she looked stuck in time. Her frozen body fell to the floor, and all laughter halted.

"Dora, Dora WTF?" Bodies began to hover around her. She was now foaming slightly from her mouth, her breathing was shallow, and her skin was beginning to lose color. Nip ran out to call for a C.O. and nurse, who was in no apparent rush to see what happened. Nip then went to the bathroom and began flushing the toilet, but I didn't think much of it. Another three minutes passed. The nurse was busy arguing with an inmate that she had been doing this for fifteen years and knew how to do her job. When she arrived at the scene, Izzy, another inmate, was performing CPR on Dora's lifeless body. Breathing no longer existed nor did any color to her flesh. Dora was ice blue. The nurse must have realized the urgency at that moment because you could see the terror in her eyes. Trying to remain calm, she called for backup, and in another two minutes came a stretcher with three more medics. Immediately, they lifted her body and took her out.

That was the last time we saw her. Dora had overdosed from fentanyl. I had already been prepared that MSC would be in effect for the rest of the night. As I sadly began to walk back toward my cubicle shocked by what I'd just witnessed, in marched about eight officers. I know what happened was absolutely terrible, but I didn't think it deserved a 'fogging,' but all officers were geared with elastic gloves which usually meant things were about to be confiscated.

"Shake-down, ladies. One bitch One bunk" yelled one man. *Yes, they really talked to us like that.*

Two officers stood in the center of the room watching all movement like hawks. We had to sit on our hands on our beds and not move. Anybody with bunks toward the back had to sit at the tables with hands palm-down. I had no idea what was going on, but obediently, I sat on my hands, wondering. Three lady officers walked to the bathroom area and called each inmate one by one. Meanwhile four officers ran through our totes. It was a house raid all over again. There was no respect or diligence shown for our items. As they ripped and rampaged our things, it was my turn to go to the bathroom.

It was a strip search. We had to derobe to our bare bones. I bent over to touch my toes and coughed. Taking my clothes, she shook everything, ran my pockets, and then combed her fingers through my hair, which was in braids. I stood cold and exposed, ashamed, and I hadn't even committed a crime. She threw the clothes back at me, which I took personally, and told me, "Dress."

I was escorted back to my bunk to assume my position.

About an hour or so later, the shake-down ceased. All extra totes, blankets and sheets had been taken, but the drugs, which I discovered was what they were after, were not found. To my surprise, Nip didn't even have a look of worry on her face, but I already knew why. She had just gotten away with murder, literally.

When I was finally able to get to the phone again, I began a conversation with my mother regarding the business.

"How are we looking?"

'Everything is fine. Don't worry about it" was the response I got to almost every business-related question. I trusted that although I knew better. Besides, there wasn't much I could do. I wasn't sure how this entire thing was going to pan out, and the company was the main and only financial source for my mother. We could not afford things to be halted for the sake of the state. To take precautions, I thought of a plan around it. Getting in touch with my accountant, we dissolved my tea company and opened another company under my mother. This would ensure that if the company was to be under investigation, it could be conducted without interrupting funds. All of this was perfectly legal, and I felt a little accomplished knowing that the family would still be taken care of in case the worst were to happen. Jamal, my accountant, kept me in the loop and alerted me once the process was complete.

Days had passed, and Jamal finally filled me in on our numbers. Yet another surprise—they were not looking good at all. We were super short on our goals, and money was unaccounted for. Hearing this information was devastating. All that we'd worked for, that I had worked for, seemingly, was going down the drain.

Michelle's fourth birthday was just days away, the business was failing, and I couldn't seem to get anyone to focus. I felt hopeless and quite frankly didn't care about it or anything else, for that matter. I had concluded that this business was part of the reason I was confined to this hell hole. It had caused great pain in my marriage and missed time with my children. I was aching for time I couldn't get back, and my business was at the center of it. *Why couldn't I get a regular job like other Americans? In fact, that's what I'll do. I'll get a nine-to-five like everyone else. I'll cook dinner for the family. We can be normal. We will be fine.* I was tired and really just wanted to get a break, so convincing myself seemed right. I had made my mind up and was going to fill my mother in on my new plan to gift her the business to run as she pleased, and I would go back into the medical field to a twenty-eight dollar an hour job, which wasn't that bad.

Jamal and I had become close over the last few calls, as we spoke a lot about business. He was not only my accountant, but a good friend, as well as a savvy businessman himself. He would often tell me about his business ventures and problems he was facing. I was able to help problem-solve, not being directly connected, and vice versa. With the new plan in mind, I wanted to bounce it off someone. David was still in *I don't want to talk to you over this phone* mode, and the girls weren't business minded. Jamal, to be honest, was like my confidant, and I felt abandoned by David. One evening, I broke down to him. I expressed my frustration with the business and my plan to give up. I expressed my feelings as a failed mother and neglectful wife. I said that I wanted to be better and that I could just be normal. I wanted out. I used the entire fifteen minutes to vent, and before he could respond, I needed to double clip. I did, which of course, bought backlash, but I didn't care. The next fifteen were words I needed to hear.

"New, you're kidding me, right? You sound real soft right now. *I could just be normal,*" he mocked. "Think about this. You're in jail right now, and you are still providing for your family. How many people do you know can say that? You're the chosen one, and that means shit will get tough sometimes, but you're made for this. From the moment I met you, I knew you were special. You had in you what I don't see in none of these so-called 'entrepreneurs' out here. You've put in the work, and you're leaving a legacy for your children so they can have what you didn't. That normal shit is for normal people. You are not built like that. Put your cape back on and handle that shit before I bang you in the mouth." He was joking, but his tone was firm.

I wanted to roll my eyes, curse him out, laugh, and cry all at once. So I said nothing.

He was right!

He continued on to talk about other business partners he worked with, making comparisons and further explaining how great of a person he thought I was. He broke down what a normal life could look like, and that just about did it for me. By time the fifteen was over, I had a restored hope for the future. I wasn't sure how, but I knew that I wasn't about to fall victim to my situation. Jamal had found my dying flame, and I was more than grateful for his time. Calling him became routine at a point, bouncing new ideas and catching up on his personal life. It helped time pass less painfully. Fifteen minutes flew by with every conversation.

I'm honestly not sure what I would have done without him, because he kept me grounded. Business talk kept my wheels turning in a stagnant place like this, and anytime we did get personal, it helped me feel less caged. I found myself looking forward to any phone conversation we did have. When I got off the phone, I was recharged. I immediately went into boss mode. When the lights cut off, I made myself a cup of coffee. I secretly felt like a trader; drinking coffee seemed like the lesser of two evils. I pulled out my pen and pad, and I went to town. I stayed up, literally all night conjuring up a new plan. I was determined not to let New Secrets Tea fail. I came up with a goal and how to delegate appropriately. I calculated numbers as provided by Jamal and set deadlines. I wrote contracts, financial breakdowns, inventory needs, and devised a marketing plan. It was no wonder they were calling for breakfast and I had yet to see the back of my eyelids. Beginning to tire, I finally ran out of ideas, but was more than ready to implement. I had about three hours before the phone cut on, so I would need to quickly eat and rest if I was going to be first on the phone.

I guess because I was tired my patience was a little low, but right at that moment two White girls walked past. I overheard one say, "Nigga, please."

Now I know these two girls aren't "racist," but something about it didn't sit well with me. Without thought of what I was actually going to say, I walked to the front of the room and grabbed our makeshift microphone made of the cardboard of the tissue paper and a cup.

"Attention A dorm... Good morning..." After a slight pause, I continued, "This message is for all my White girls, so listen up. I understand you may not be racist, and I don't care how many Black friends you have, if you have mixed kids, or if your boyfriends are Black. If your birth certificate says White or Caucasian, you are not permitted to say Nigga. That's with a 'g g a' or a 'g g e r.' They are both inappropriate and offensive. If you say it around me, I will smack the shit out of you, and I'm not playing."

Now, if compassion had a "street" version, I'm almost certain this is it. The way these White girls used that word so casually was offensive, and I truly believe a warning was wayyyyy sweet.

The entire dorm had shocked faces, and I have to be honest, I was a little shocked myself, but it was already done. I had had enough, and It was time to set some boundaries. I was tired of remaining quiet for the sake of someone else's perception of me. I was tired of having a voice and not being heard. I decided to have this revelation in the middle of prison to a bunch of individuals who didn't care if I lived or died, and it baffled even me. But that didn't stop the ball of emotions being silenced since childhood from welling up past my ears, and projectile vomiting words to a half-awake crowd.

"Furthermore," I continued and walked over to the phone list I was on for the evening and ripped it off the wall. "I will be taking over this phone. If that's a problem, we can step to the back." There was silence. I didn't mean any disrespect to anyone, and I damn sure did not want to fight, but I think I was just at breaking point and needed some change.

"Y'all have a good morning and thank you." I smiled and put the microphone back. A couple inmates clapped and shouted, and one inmate came and hugged me. I quietly ate my food and went to bed. I had to catch this catnap before it was time to revive New Secrets Tea. I quadruple clipped that morning: I called my mom and broke down her tasks, David was assigned inventory and marketing, Donna got email research and wholesale catalog duty, and Jamal had numbers to crunch. I provided deadlines in which I would follow up with each and expressed my gratitude. It was game time, and if we were going to save the business, all hands were needed on deck.

- OM: THE SELF WITHIN -

> "Forgiveness is the fragrance that the violet sheds on the heel that has crushed it."
>
> - Mark Twain -

16

Kshama

THE ACT OF PATIENCE, RELEASING TIME, AND THE CAPACITY TO FORGIVE

I HADN'T RECEIVED COMMISSARY money for several weeks because everyone was so 'busy.' Because of that, I started as a worker for the jail. I was assigned bathrooms and showers. For a dollar a day, I would scrub all six bathrooms and seven showers. For the most part, it didn't bother me because it became routine and occupied my mind. It was only the times when there was literal shit or a toilet overflowed because someone tried to flush their crusty drawers. For the life of me I didn't understand the mentality of some of these so-called women. For seven dollars a week, I had to deal with used tampons left in the sink, but we were on a four-day streak of normal bathroom usage.

The business was being taken care of, and I could contact them as much as I needed now that I ran one of the phones, so things were looking up, all things considered. I was in such high spirits that I decided to roam the dayroom a little, busting ass in a few games of spade and 5000. Dare I say, I was starting to get a little comfortable. The cold didn't bother me as much, often walking around in wife beaters and thermal leggings, both the rebels and the officers were predictable, making it easy to read them, and even the food started to be consumable. Not quite at the enjoyable level just yet, but getting close.

Berry and Rico, my Puerto Rican princesses, decided that tonight we would celebrate a little. Rico was going to pour us up some hooch, which is jail wine made from base, sugar, bread, and fruit. She had been burping this batch over two months now, so it was ready for consumption. It smelled of actual alcohol, and I had slight excitement. Hooch was considered a contraband, and although correctional officers knew we made it, if we were openly caught with it we could get a ticket. So while Berry and Rico were pouring our cups with their backs toward the open, I didn't think anything of it. Precaution was best; we made a hookup which was noodles with some concoction of meat and cheese. Tonight's hookup was tacos, cheesy noodles with pulled buffalo chicken, pepperoni, nacho crumbles, dried pickles, and cream cheese on top. It never sounded appetizing, but for the most part, it was always delicious. Good energy was flowing, and for the first time in my jail experience, I was feeling grateful. I had never felt so sure of myself as I did at that moment. All I could do was smile and thank God that I had lived to see another day. Berry had previously done a few other jailhouse tattoos and while I played cards, one of her works slid across my eye view. It sparked an idea.

"Berry, I want a quick tattoo," I found myself saying.

Again with the decision-making thing. Listen, I was in a very low vibrational space, and I didn't feel like I had much to lose. What were they going to do? Throw me in jail? haha

I hadn't thought too much about it, but I had made up my mind earlier that I no longer wanted to live a life of regret. I wanted to take actions that made me happy and fearless. I was tired of living under the expectations of others; I wanted to be free. This was my first act of freedom, I thought to myself. I already knew what I wanted because of the meaning. I wanted the sixth chakra symbol, the third eye, which meant true knowledge of self. What better symbol? I was to put it right behind my ear. I didn't think the location out too well, but I was satisfied. Berry grabbed her needle, wiped it with alcohol, burned it with a lighter and wiped it again, probably not the most sanitary experience which I knew from my medical background, but it was jail, and I didn't expect anything else. I was committed. She gave me my drink, I sat between her legs, and as I slow sipped, she went to town on my neck, dipping the needle in black ink from a pen and poking it into my skin. It hurt, of course, but it wasn't a pain I couldn't tolerate. Plus, several inmates were engaged, so I couldn't back out now. About thirty to forty-five minutes later, she was done. The tattoo looked absolutely nothing like what it was supposed to, and I died laughing when I saw it in the mirror. That was exactly what I got, but I could only find humor in the situation. I was okay with it, though. It was an experience that nobody could take from me. Furthermore, it was the symbolism that counted for me. My act of freedom was ingrained on my neck for life. The hooch tasted a lot like fermented sangria, with the fruit being the most potent. It was good, but I'm not sure I would say I enjoyed it. Towards the end it got much more bitter, so I downed it to get it over with. No sooner than I did that, Berry and Rico had a devilish smile on their faces.

"WTF y'all ugly tails looking at?" I said, laughing.

"I spiked our drinks with about thirty pills of Zoloft. We going to be up tonight." She laughed and started dancing. Instantly my face dropped. Zoloft is an antidepressant, which means it's an 'upper.' It gets the heart pumping, and with a heart murmur it scares the crap out of me.

"Yeah, we basically just took a molly!" Rico high-fived Berry. That's all she popped uptown, so it was a real party for her. I was having a baby heart attack and was livid all in one. I explained I had a heart murmur and why that wasn't cool. You could see the regret on their faces, but it was too late now. At that moment, one of the cool C.O.s came in, her name was Basket. She was a chocolate thing with a gorgeous smile. Rico had the biggest crush on her, and of all days, she chose today to come and play spades with the three of us. I tried to play it off as much as possible because I didn't want to get Berry or Rico in trouble. Basket was around my age, so I'm sure by my uncontrollable hand tremors, she knew something was up. But she never acknowledged it. So we kept playing.

At this point, my heart was fluttering at a pace that terrified me. I downed a bunch of water in hopes to wash it all away. But it didn't help. I had to ride it out, and that I did.

I was up for two days straight. My hands would not stop shaking, and I looked like someone with a bad case. Every time I went to lay down, I felt my heart skip a beat or two, frightening the holy hell out of me. I was so concentrated on not passing the heck out or worse. Berry and Rico went to sleep just fine, leaving me to fend for myself through the nights. That made me mad too.

Why couldn't I stop shaking? And why would people volunteer to do this to themselves? Drugs are dumb!!! I had decided by the end of day two, I was finally able to ride the high. I could finally lie down long enough without the feeling of an oncoming heart attack, and things were starting to feel better. I had put a tent up, which meant hanging a blanket to block the view of my bed, to block the light. I wasn't able to sleep just yet, but I knew I would be welcoming it with open arms sooner or later. I lay in my tent, quiet and ready to meet my eyelids.

Before I knew it, Rico popped her head in.

"Newnew, you okay?" She sounded concerned.

"Yeah, it's starting to wear off now. I'll be good."

She had climbed into the tent at this point. "Aww, I feel so bad. We shouldn't have done that. We just thought it was going to be fun, and we knew you would say no. My bad, boo." She began to rub my back, which felt amazing. Rico had informed me she was a massage therapist uptown, and right now, she was absolutely believable.

"Want me to help you sleep?" she inquired. Little did she know, another three minutes on my back at this rate would have me out like a light.

"Uh huh" was all I could muster up. She straddled me and went to town. The combination of being so tired and being high, the massage was heightened. I almost forgot I was in a tent in jail for a second. She worked from my neck to my back, down my butt and into my thighs. She did this for some time, and I melted a little more with each stroke. For the first night here, I got some good sleep.

> "I think the first step is to understand that forgiveness does not exonerate the perpetrator. Forgiveness liberates the victim. It's a gift you give yourself."
>
> - T. D. Jakes -

My birth control that had been in my arm had expired back in November of last year. I had been complaining of numbness to my arm for over two months now, and the OBGYN kept putting me off. Her excuse was that surgical tools are not allowed in the prison because we are criminals. This meant I would need to be taken to the university. Unfortunately, that is a process in itself, because I would need to be escorted by guards and specially treated. We weren't allowed to be near the general population. Both wardens from either location had to approve the transition and so forth. In other words, it was a long way of saying, *It's not a priority and we will get to you when we see fit*. Once I began to take the complaints and annoyance up several notches, I began to get results. I wrote grievances every single day. I knew it wouldn't mean much, but at least it would be on the books.

After all of that, it was finally time. They called me to the OBGYN office and told me she would be removing it right here. Another chance at seeing daylight gone right before my eyes, and I had a feeling I would never see daylight again. What was most scary was that I was becoming okay with that. It was the new norm. Nonetheless, I entered the room and was greeted by Dr. Joyner.

"Mrs. Jones. Yes! We are going to try to remove your NEXPLANON today. I have the surgical tools they approved, and we are going to see what we can do," she stated.

"You're going to try?" were my first words.

The nurse butted in. "She's a doctor."

"Those were her words, not mine. Someone saying try isn't very comforting," I protested with a smile. Regardless, this object needed to be removed.

"You're right. I shouldn't have used those words. We are going to get it," she said in her Indian accent. She was a cute and small older lady probably in her late fifties, early sixties. She was the first and only medical staff I came across who seemed to care for us as humans and not untamed animals. Although I was skeptical, I liked her, so I let my guard down a little. She got me up on the chair after first trying to decide which way she wanted me to lie. Once settled, she wiped my arm with alcohol. The nurse opened the supplies. She was poking at the small rod in my arm as if to see how to remove it. She then took an orange permanent marker to make a spot to make an incision.

"Don't you think you should use gloves?" I inquired, after which she stopped and put them on. I rolled my eyes, beginning to regret my decision, but once again, I was in too deep to stop now. I was told by the nurse several times to look away, and to be honest, I wanted to, but I absolutely couldn't. I had to witness what exactly was happening to my arm. She first numbed me locally, then made a small incision, then a little larger, and again sliced it wider. By the time she was done, there was a hole the size of a quarter in my arm. She tried to use the forceps to pull out the white object but couldn't seem to grab at it. It had been in my arm for three years, so of course there was fat and tissue surrounding the NEXPLANON, as expected. As I had previously seen on YouTube and other surgery removal videos, she was to grab the object by the tip and slowly rotate, and the birth control would slide right out. I could not believe my eyes at what happened next.

She had gotten ahold of a small piece of the rod. She pulled, and because it didn't move, she decided to cut at it. She took the small scapula, and as if it was meat on a bone, scraped the fat and tissue from the piece with several slices. My eyes grew wide because I just knew I was going to feel this later. After several attempts at sawing the piece out, I guess she ran out of patience. She then ripped the NEXPLANON from my arm, which I felt all the way down to my fingers.

"Ahh!" I flinched, but the nurse was busy looking for gauze to stop all the blood oozing onto the table. I let out a slight chuckle because I knew this was so incredibly wrong, and once again, it was what I got for not trusting my gut. She instructed the nurse to use the forceps to push the fat back into my body as she used sterile strips to try to tape me back together. By this time, I was without words. She put twenty strips on my arm, which again I knew was incorrect.

As she washed her hands, she said, "Mrs. Jones, thank you so much for your patience. This was my first NEXPLANON removal."

I simply shook my head and walked out, ashamed that I was an experiment.

That night, at medication time, I was supposed to begin receiving pain medication. When I went to the window to ask what I was getting, she said it was Flagyl, an antibiotic.

"For what?" I asked.

"You must have told her you had something." Flagyl was for yeast infections or other vaginal problems, none of which I had. I had just about had it with the medical department.

This was not the first time the medical staff was accused of giving the wrong medication. In fact it was something that occurred at least once a day. In fact, there was a whole episode with one inmate and the nurse staff. In short, the inmate was going back and forth that the medicine was not her's. The conversation got heated and before you knew it, the nurse had taken off her wig and began twirling it like a helicopter, taunting the inmate. The staff served us behind a window, so of course the inmate couldn't get her hands on her. It was extremely unprofessional and I was embarrassed even though I had nothing to do with it.

I decided I had to take matters into my own hands. I used my commissary to purchase what I needed to properly care for my wound as painlessly as possible. I got things like bacitracin and hydrocortisone. Occasionally I would get a penicillin or ibuprofen to stop an infection or dull the radiating pain running from my neck to my fingers. The wound was still open and bleeding, so I had to steal bandages and gauze from the nurse's office whenever I went to talk to the guards. The hustle had to be real because in this place, you were susceptible to catch anything, and I mean anything.

In the real world, we had to prepare to move from our previous home. We were not allowed to be there during an active case, and rent was incredibly high to pay to reside there. We had to arrange for movers to come, pack our things, and put it all in a POD. David's childhood friend was to be there to help orchestrate it all, but it was a hard pill to swallow to have to arrange such a task over the phone. David was still restrained to home detention, so his help was also limited. Not to mention, David's grandfather, who had also been like a grandfather to me considering I never had one, had just passed away. It was something I had feared from the time Keva discovered her child was shot on TV that one night. It was the most helpless I had felt this entire time. I found it ironic that throughout David and my ten-year relationship, every time we went to separate, one of our family members died. First his father then my grandmother, and he was actually in the house about to break up with me the night my stepfather passed.

This time, he was once again grieving, and I could not be there to help him get through. On top of that, this was our children's first death experience. I was certain Michael was unaffected, but Michelle understood for the most part. She kept telling me that Baba was crying when we would talk. She said that she would rub his back and say it would be okay. I knew that her love was carrying him through, but all I could do was pray. I couldn't even provide words of comfort. This was the hardest task to accomplish since I had gotten here, and through it all, I just wanted to wrap my arms around him and tell him it would be okay. You could hear in his voice that he was trying to hold it together, but he was shattered. It pained me to even call, so when I did I made sure to pray.

I again prayed for his strength and courage. I prayed for his understanding and most importantly, his peace. None of this had been easy on him. And although I had my feelings on everything, I knew that David's love for me was truly unconditional. He might not have expressed it the way I wanted, but he expressed it the best way he knew how, and I was ever grateful for that. He was an amazing man but never really had an outlet to express his grievances. He was just expected to provide even when his true feelings and desires were never considered. I had realized that from sitting in this hellhole, and I just wished there was a way to tell him he was more than appreciated as a Black man and father.

So I just continued to pray. I had to forgive him for all I held against him even if he was a liar and cheater! I also prayed that he could find it in his heart to forgive me. Even though he had hurt me, the truth is, we need our Black men and should build them up way more than we break them down.

"Be thankful for what you have; you'll end up having more. If you concentrate on what you don't have, you will never, ever have enough."

- Oprah Winfrey -

17

Dhanya Vad
TO FEEL GRATITUDE

MARCH WAS ONLY a few weeks away, and my heart began to fill with anxiety because I didn't know what would happen. I had no doubt in my mind that I would eventually be set free, but my fear was that I would be postponed first. It was happening to everyone. I had a ninety-day hit, which meant every postponement would be another three months. The thought made me sick to my stomach, but every time I got like that, I would stop and pray. They say if you pray don't worry, and if you worry don't pray. Of course it was easier said than done, but I was sticking to it.

Today we got the opportunity to go to the gym. This was something we were supposed to do every week, yet I didn't even know we had one. This was my fifth month, and I had yet to see the gym. I couldn't wait to hit the treadmill or lift some weights. I imagined it looked just like the gym in the prison yards with some free weights and bench press bars lying around. The only catch to go be able to go was ... it was all or nothing. Every inmate in the dorm had to go, or nobody could go. It was about sixty of us at this point, and all but about twelve wanted in. Berry and I had been here the longest at this point. Over time, we'd gained the respect of the majority of the dorm. Mostly due to seniority, but also because she was known to fix the phones, and I was known to fix a problem. We held things down, Berry and I. Plus these were all new faces, so what we said went—Rules of the Jungle! We both wanted to see something different, so we rounded them up.

"Y'all got five minutes, or we literally will fight and then drag you out. We all have to go. Majority rules, so get your asses up. This is not a drill, people. Let's move it. You don't have to exercise, but your ass gotta go. Don't make it hard, just line up at the back, people. Let's go!" I was yelling in the middle of the room, disregarding the eye rolls and grunts while Berry went to shake those who were pretending to sleep. It took a couple threats, but eventually we got everyone on board and heading to the back of the dorm. We went through a door that had been locked since I'd gotten here. Through that door was another door we walked through to outside. It was an open space with about four basketball hoops. There were four phones on the side, and it was caged in, but it was outside. I was so happy to see sunlight that I completely bypassed the fact that it was only about forty degrees out here. I stopped and took a big breath. Who knew freedom was just right on the other side of that door?

WOW! Fresh air, something I hadn't had since October 2018. The sky was blue and bright, and the sun was shining. I leaped for joy. Literally! I ran like a little schoolgirl in circles and leaped like a ballerina several times. The rest of the crowd kept it moving through another set of doors which lead to an indoor version of the same thing. There were no weights or benches. Only two deflated basketballs, four hoops, four phones, a table with a radio, and several chairs. I played a round of ball, three on three, in which I was impressed that I still had my shot from high school. I laughed until it hurt from happiness. I danced when some music came on 92Q and although I didn't know any of the songs playing, I didn't care at all if I was making a fool of myself. Any other time I would have frozen at the thought of shooting hoops and missing in front of people to just let my little kid out period, but I didn't care. I was in a space of joy, and it came from the inside. Eventually, I found myself playing another game outside because our blood was pumping so much we were actually hot.

"First to five," making it a quick game. The final shot was a three pointer I shot for shits and giggles. *Swish* I sunk the shot and dropped to the floor in laughter. I laid there for a good five minutes, ceasing laughter but focused on the sky.

I closed my eyes and took in the warmth, meditating for a few breaths.

The cold on my nose was refreshing. I knew God was watching me. I knew He was there, I felt him. It was as if He wrapped his arms around me and gave a squeeze. A tear welled in my eyes. I felt peace. Just then, I knew everything was going to be okay. Regardless of how it all turned out, God's got me. He sees me, even right now!

Before the tears could form and fall, the C.O. interrupted.

"Jones, get up! It's time to go!" I was sad it was over but grateful it happened. As I slowly walked back to the cell walls, I took a moment to reflect. I couldn't remember the last time I just looked up at the sky and was truly thankful for a shining sun beating down on my beautiful brown skin. I smiled, taking in my newfound appreciation for something as simple as having a moment of fresh air, something I'd never said thank you for. This was the start of my gratitude practice, the act of showing this attitude of gratitude, truly appreciating what you have with 100 percent genuine contentment.

I headed back through the double doors. I had walked right back into the mess.

Blue, a local gang member, had witnessed Macy throw up a sign in the gym. Apparently, Macy was telling people she was a part of the crew. When Blue approached her to ask her, "What's the song?" Macy was silent. Macy was not aware that Blue was a member and now had two minutes to remember the 'song.' It was evident that Macy was all show, and without hesitation, Blue plucked her right in her mouth. You could hear the thud, and instantly blood was leaking from her nose or mouth or maybe both.

"Don't say that shit, if you ain't bout it," she spat as she walked away. Macy had to be G checked, and I just wanted to go home. I crawled into my bed and closed my eyes, holding on to the moment of peace I had experienced just five minutes ago.

It was 4:30, and the phones were due to cut back on. I hopped on first because I wanted to share with someone that I'd seen the sun today. My first ring was to Jamal. Strangely, he didn't answer. Thinking nothing of it, I called my mom. She answered for the first time with joy. It was like she already knew what I was going to say.

"Hey, my beautiful girl." She didn't hesitate. "Guess what?" she blurted. We were clearly both bursting with stories to tell. "You're coming home ... Friday! We got you an early date. Isn't that such good news?"

"Wait, what?" My heart started to beat fast.

I knew that she wouldn't say it unless it was true, but I still didn't want to get my hopes up. I had been let down too many times to do this again. I wanted this to be true so bad, I completely forgot about my sun story.

"What are you saying?" I stuttered.

"You heard me right. The judge approved the request today. Not sure what all of that means nor can we discuss it over the phone, but you're coming home."

I didn't need to hear anymore. Today had been a good day, and I officially would be home in just two days. I hung up with the biggest smile on my face, and nothing could change my mood. Not even the fact that Jamal didn't answer the three more calls placed that night or the three-woman fight that caused yet another fog.

Today was the day. It had been six months, and I was finally heading home. I woke up early and got dressed, waiting for my name to be called for court. I ate breakfast, bright-eyed and bushy-tailed. I even ate my court bag, a bag with two hard-boiled eggs, a box of cereal, and a carton of cow's milk. Our C.O. began calling the names out. She finished her list and turned to walk out.

"C.O., wait, wait, wait," I yelled desperately. "You didn't call my name."

"That's because you're not on the list."

"Check again. I'm supposed to go to court. You see, my lawyer—"

She cut me off. "You're not listed, Jones. Move along."

Here we go with this shit again. They loaded the court ladies onto the elevator. As the door slowly closed, all hope of leaving today went with it. I knew what was said, but something wasn't right. Hours had passed and nothing. As soon as the phones cut on, I was on it dialing my mother. No response. I was low key freaking out. *What if they forget me? What if they lost my paperwork? Will I ever get out of here? Maybe I had a warrant out that they didn't mention?* By noon, I just went back to bed. This was home now, so I might as well face it.

I didn't try calling again until the 4:30 phone. By then I had already expected I wasn't going home. My heart hurt too much to even care.

When my mom picked up, she got to explaining. I stopped her ... with very little strength in my voice.

"It's cool, Mom. I'd rather not talk about it anymore. I'd rather not know. I'd rather not be let down anymore. I just want to sit quietly for a while."

Before hanging up, she was compelled to tell me that they were unsure who, but someone dropped the ball. Everyone was in court today, and the judge was pissed because I was not there. It brought me no extra comfort knowing that I truly could have been going home today if only people cared enough to make sure all steps were taken, but it was water under the bridge now, so I didn't bother following up with any questions. She told me it was unknown when my new date would be set.

Disheartened, I hung up, and quickly double-clipped to call Jamal. He still didn't respond. Now I was starting to worry. I could tell in my gut something was off.

But I was in jail, clearly not getting out any time soon. I crawled into bed completely broken. Why did God allow this to happen? Why was I in here and my husband was in the world? Why was he able to hold our children and eat real food, and I was caged like a wild animal? When would I see daylight unmonitored and at my own free will?

As these thoughts began to swirl in my mind, I had to put a stop to it. I realized it was only going to put me in a negative and depressed state. I began to think about the sun. Something I never thought about before. I thought about how great it felt on my skin. How it seemed to hug me and provide comfort. I thought about the cold yet fresh air that I was still able to breathe in, and how many people didn't wake up that morning to have another breath. I thought about the food I am able to taste, even when it may not taste good. I just began to dwell on all the little things that I need to be grateful for. Yes - I wanted to sit on what was wrong, but the truth was, that little hour of gym time put some things into perspective.

That night, or morning rather, when I went to shower at 3am, I knew the time would be when all my bunkmates had gone for their methadone treatment. I found myself yet again, crying in the shower. I shed so many tears, I had no idea what was from me or from the rusting shower head. I closed my eyes and just released. There was a sound that came from the pit of my soul. A fire or burning, or maybe it was heartburn, but something was shuffling in my chest. I only could hold my heart as I sobbed so hard that my head hurt.

"God, please, I need you! I need you!"

I must have said this 100 times, but it was all my mouth could bear.

"Please help me! I can't do this without you, Please give me strength" I bellowed, wanting nothing more than for Him to show face right there. I, literally, balled up into what felt like nothing, hugging my knees, but still aware that lying on the floor would most definitely render an infection.

I was in the shower over 45 minutes for sure, and I only knew because an episode of scandal had come and gone. I lay in my bunk, still broken, but I was all dried up by this time. I had shed so many tears that my eyes were puffy and red, and my tear ducts were empty. The rest of the weekend carried on. I skipped all my meals this time. I wasn't fasting, I just had no room for food. I felt empty but wasn't hungry. I did make a taco hookup during the midnight hour.

Monday morning came around, and my belly began to rumble. I decided I would force myself to eat. I got up to one of the better meals, sweet rice and scrambled egg powder. As I ate with very little life in my body, I heard a C.O. entering the dorm.

"Jones ... Court," she yelled.

I heard her but didn't really register anything, especially since I hadn't heard that I would be going.

She yelled again. "Jones ... get dressed."

My bunkmate shoved me. "Newnew - get your ass up, bitch."

I stumbled across the dorm searching for my court clothes, which was merely another pink jumpsuit with a little more crisp to it. Quickly brushing my teeth, I headed toward the lobby praying that they weren't wrong but secretly feeling like they would soon tell me to turn around.

Feeling like a criminal escaping prison, I boarded the elevator and stood to the side, head down, excited that my plan to escape was possibly happening.

I made it. Five floors down. Level one. The doors opened, and there it was, a glass window that led to the outside. On the left, a gate with four guards standing on the other side. I stopped and looked to the right. A fleeting thought occurred.

Just run. It's right there. Run.

The thought went just as fast as it came as soon as I noticed the three other guards and the long driveway to the gate. I wasn't making it anywhere without permission. I walked left, and the standing guards began to bark commands.

"Arms up. Turn around. Stand on the wall. Take off your clothes. Touch your toes. Cough. Spread your legs. Lift your arms. Show your panties. Shake your socks. Open your mouth. Lift your tongue." It kept coming.

There was no please or thank you. They had no gentleness about them, and these were the women. After being searched, they formed us into a line and cuffed us with one chain dangling down past our ankles. We were shoved into a room with a cement block for a bench, where we were cuffed above our ankles. The cuffs were fastened so tight that it hurt to walk. It felt like with each step, the metal was cutting into my Achilles. I knew that my legs would be bleeding in a matter of time.

With no jackets, because the men took them, we stepped into the cold and frosty March air. I once again did not mind the coldness. It was a gloomy day, so the warmth from the sun did not exist like the day at the gym, but it was appreciated.

We stepped into a van, not much warmer than outside, but the seats were cushioned, so once again I felt a wave of appreciation flush over my body. As we rode through the city, the other girls were joking back and forth. One girl, who was clearly still high from her dose of methadone, was joking around with the people, calling them bitches, but most of us ignored her with the exception of her use of the 'N' word, where even I cut in to tell her *Don't try it*. Intentionally, looking through the window I sat next to, their voices became distant noise. I was seeing the city for what felt like the first time. We made three stops before arriving at Mitchell, an old courthouse with a vintage feel. We were shoved through a door to the noise cell, where at least 20 male inmates were held yelling their court related thoughts back and forth. Mimi, a small Black lady about the age of 64, with very small dreads and a gold tooth, who just two days ago had gotten caught trying to steal my book, and I were shoved into a 3x5 cell.

Mimi began to ramble on about topics I could not tell you about. My mind was racing, and I had no patience to try to figure out how to make small talk. A few hours passed, and I was finally called. I got up from the only small crate in the closet that I had balled myself on top of and came to the gate.

It was my lawyer. He told me that everything was going to be okay. He explained that I had two options.

Being that they had no evidence against me, I would most certainly beat the case. He explained that I could continue to plead not guilty and take it to trial. He followed up that I would be in jail until such time. Because I still had 2 postponements that they could take, I would most likely be there for another 6 months, but I would not be convicted. My second option would give me a record and I could later expunge it. However, this option would send me home today.

Without even a second thought, I said, "I want to go home!"

He nodded his head and left. Another 20-30 minutes rolled by before I heard my name again. This time they were opening the gated door. I was being dragged down a long hallway and up 56 steps. I counted. Each step was slower than the one before because the cuffs were still slicing through my now bleeding skin.

*"When you have no judgment,
you will see others with kindness.
You choose compassion over judgment, and by doing this,
you become a conduit for peace, understanding,
and happiness.."*

- NatalieAntoinette -

18

Karuna Hu
I AM COMPASSION

SHACKLED LIKE A true slave, the guard pushed me through a door which was actually the back of the courtroom. I walked in, completely amazed at how "grand" everything appeared. A slight fear set in with the realization that I wasn't in a movie or watching a trial on TV. I wasn't in the audience supporting someone I knew. I was the only one chained in pink gear and cornrows. I was the one shoveling to the desk to stand before someone to judge me. David, who I had not seen in months, rose from the audience. He looked delicious, and I wanted nothing more than to hug him. All my harsh feelings of being abandoned disappeared. I missed him and just admired how good he looked in his gold framed glasses. To my left was my lawyer, then my husband, and then his lawyer. Three handsome Black men, dapper in their suits, crisp glasses and shiny shoes, and me. When I looked up at the judge, she had a look on her face as though she'd just caught me stealing cookies out of her cookie jar, almost motherly.

I panned away, scared to keep eye contact, and caught eyes with the two massive portraits behind her. Both White figures appeared to be staring right into my soul. A wave of dread came over me, and suddenly my breathing became shallow. I signaled to the closest guard to get me a tissue, but the idea of turning away from the judge was not pleasing to her.

I had to close my eyes and count my breath. It was the only way to calm myself down before having an uncontrollable panic attack.

She began with her routine, which I could tell she was not at all excited about. Parts of what she was saying I couldn't catch. I was still in a daze that this was all happening. The only thing that I caught was, "Judge, we are asking for a year with five years' probation."

I lost my breath completely. The tears started flowing. I was once again feeling hopeless because I knew if she heard my side, I would be freed.

"I'll give her two years," they continued, and I simply focused on my breath. I needed my lawyer to hear so he could explain it to me later.

She asked me at some point if I was guilty. I paused. I wanted to yell NO! and that she needed to understand, but nothing would come out. I knew that one wrong move could land me back in bookings, or even down the cut.

"Yes, ma'am," I mumbled, still in shock that this was my outcome.

She continued on a few more sentences and dismissed the case.

My lawyer explained, "You got a year, but since you served six months already it's considered time served. You have two years' probation with ten year backup."

"What's that mean?"

"It means that if you mess up at all during these next two years, it will be an automatic ten years in prison."

I was sick, but slightly relieved because I was finally going home. I missed my babies so much. All I could think about was when, where, and how long until I would be able to wrap my arms around them and steal kisses.

Before I could even turn to David and say anything, I was whisked away like a thief in the night, back down 56 stairs and into the very small room.

Low and behold, there was one more person in this box. It was Dro, who was sent to the cut for her PREA violation. She filled me in on who did what, the fights, the food, all the happenings down in Jessup MD. She explained how you get to go outside all the time, play video games, watch movies, and even get on Facebook. To be honest, she made prison seem almost enjoyable, certainly better than jail. She explained to me how one bunkmate who was facing life was just recently released. She had told on her codefendant and word on the street was that she had 24 hours to live.

The story made me so sick to my stomach. Here I was hemmed up with people who really did commit crimes and some who had every intention of committing more once they could, and I was being forced to plead guilty to a crime I didn't even commit. How messed up is this system?

I just wanted to go home.

A few more hours and a snack box later, we were boarding another van to return to bookings. The ladies sat, some discussing their hearings, others quiet because their hearing didn't go too well.

Drake's 'Sick of These Niggas' played on the radio. It was nice to hear music, but it let me know just how out of the loop I was. I bumped to the music anyway because the truth was, Felon or not, I was going home.

Entering back into my dorm, the ones that were up were standing, waiting to hear news. When I walked in I kept a straight-faced, trying not to prematurely give away my exciting news. I paused for dramatic effects then in one swift "nay nay" I sang "I'm going outside today" by NBA Youngboy.

A huge "Ayyee" came from my bunkmates, and I accepted my applause as I headed to my bunk to rest. I wanted to sleep until it was time to go in about 12 hours.

My final hours were the slowest ones yet. Dinner came and went, and I just couldn't sleep. I was so close I could smell it.

Of course, not everyone was happy for me. Samantha, a mother of five accused of killing one of her children, was one of them. She kept giving me an eye, which didn't bother me, but she wanted me to know.

When the phones cut on, I was still responsible. I didn't want to talk to anyone, so I thought I'd spend this time assigning the phone to someone. As my phone stayed in rotation, Samantha decided she wanted to use our line. Her name was not on my list, but she jumped one of my members, so of course I knew she was looking for trouble. I was already released to go home, so I had no problem playing with fire today. I approached her.

"Samantha, you know damn well you ain't supposed to be on my phone. You been here almost as long as me so don't play. Hang the phone up!"

"Or what?" She began punching in numbers.

I hung up her clip.

"I won't answer that." I began to reach for the phone. She pulled back.

"I'll rip this whole bitch out the wall." Wasn't long before the dorm caught on. About five girls were walking my way.

Oh shit, here we go, I thought to myself, prepared for whatever was heading my way.

They all came and stood in front of me.

"Not my Newnew," said Berry.

"Bitch, you got the wrong one," put in Rico.

"You ain't ripping shit," my seven month pregnant bunkmate followed up

To my surprise, they all were defending me. I guess I had gained that much respect that I didn't even need to fight. I was astonished because I didn't know people felt this way. In a real cynical way, I was kind of happy. I had managed to let my light shine even in the darkest place, and it was respected. That's big in the streets. I felt a little like a champion.

Smiling, I walked away, feeling untouchable.

It was now 3am, and I was still in the dorm. I was watching "Players Club" on Bounce TV because I still couldn't sleep. I had a nervous feeling that I too had a warrant and wouldn't be released. They were known for waiting until you went through your process before telling you they were going to rebook you. One girl got all the way to the parking lot before they decided to let her know. It was one of the most evil tricks I had heard this whole experience.

No less than ten minutes later, it happened.

"Jones, pack up." The words that make us all similar. It was the words we all waited to hear. I was already packed. I grabbed my bag of remaining commissary, books, and journaling and headed to the lobby. The process to leave was just as long as getting in. Shoveling between bullpens and rooms to be discharged. The last room I was given my personal items and the clothes I'd come in with. It was about 4am when the final process was completed. David's cousin C.O. met me and walked me around the corner. She led me through a door where David was on the other side. He was coming down the steps, and instantly I forgot about everything. I dropped my bag and ran up the steps into his arms. I broke down in tears, and my knees felt like rubber. I could barely breathe, and he was holding my entire weight.

As my sobbing slowed, I could hear a guard telling us to come off the steps before we fell, which actually wasn't a bad idea. I don't know what it was that made me forget all the anger I had pent up inside of me. Was it just because I was glad it was over? Happy to see a familiar face? Amnesia because I truly did love the man? Who knows?

I was just thankful for his strength, quite literally, in that moment. He gathered my items, and we headed toward the doors.

"The mind is the most powerful tool we possess.
What we think, what we concentrate on, we Become.
Once you realize this power, you are unstoppable."

- NatalieAntoinette -

19

Dharnana
CONCENTRATION

The cold air hit my face. This was it. I was finally free. I was all the way out and still wasn't sure if this was true. Everything was happening in slow motion. The streets were quiet, and I could hear my breath. I walked to the middle of the streets and lay down on the yellow lines. Once again my eyes were watching God. Silent tears began to flow down my face.

I'm not sure how long I was there, but eventually David interrupted.

"Baby, come on. Let's get you to a nice hot shower. And what would you like to eat?"

That was all I needed to hear. I instantly popped up.

"I've never wanted to hear that line so bad."

The only thing open was McDonalds, which I would never eat, but in this case, I happily made an exception. It couldn't be any worse than the crap I'd been eating the last six months. We grabbed a Big Mac with extra sauce, large fries, and an Oreo milkshake.

Completely satisfied, I was happy and ready to head home.

David drove us to a fancy hotel that I never even caught the name of. It really didn't matter, because even Motel 6 would have hot water, an amenity I will never take for granted again.

The hotel room was immaculate. A massive king bed, huge flat screen, and of course an overhead shower. David's mother had sent a gift bag. It was a duffle bag of smell goods, bath gels, lotions, perfumes. She had purchased me three pairs of underwear and a bra, pajamas, a sweater, jeans, and a pair of boots. When I saw the bag, once again tears flowed. Partly because I was so appreciative of everything before me. Partly because everything before me was now all that I had to my name.

"Thank you, God."

I must have taken at least an hour in the shower and used probably half of my gel. I was just oozing at the aromas. I couldn't get enough.

By time I came from the shower, David had two glasses of my favorite wine and a movie on the FireStick ready. Another moment of gratitude.

We never actually got to the movie. We stared at each other for a while and then began to share stories of the last few months. My stories were not any more interesting although I was actually behind bars. Things were just as crazy on the outside. A piece of me almost felt bad because of all the stress he had been forced to face alone.

This moment quickly left when I suggested we make love. His response was not one I expected.

"Let me find a condom. I don't want another baby." Now logically, this made sense. We were not in a position that another baby would bring joy. However, it turned me completely off. How could that be the words to me when I was his wife, who he hadn't seen in over six months? Call it emotional, but I was hurt.

"What the hell do you mean?" I started, knowing that the outcome would not lead to sex. The remainder of the night was full of tension. We argued over our feelings and how we both felt neglected, neither one of us really hearing the other because the topic was too sore.

Before we knew it, it was 7:30am and time for me to go check in with my new probation officer. The conversation was left open with no real conclusion decided. It was the start of the unknown for this relationship.

I spent the next few hours at the P.O.'s office, waiting to be explained the rules and expectations of what the next two years would look like.

"You will report once a week. Traveling must be approved by the courts, and any violation will put you right back in prison for a minimum of ten years," she said in a real mundane type of voice. You could tell she had been doing this for years and probably didn't enjoy it. You could also tell she wasn't the P.O. that you wanted to test. Something about her read *Rule Enforcer* all over.

I took a drug test and then was dismissed. No sooner than 10am did I get a call from my mother.

"Hey baby girl. Oh I'm so glad to be able to call your phone to hear you. I've missed you so much" she began. "Listen, the airport is blowing up my phone. They know you've been released and are trying to reach you. We are way behind on rent and sales have been extremely low. Any idea how you want to handle this?"

I was out all of six hours and it was already time for business. I regretfully opened my email, only to find 352 unopened emails, 69 of which were from the last week alone. The most recent was from the airport requesting to schedule a meeting asap. Knowing I couldn't avoid this much longer, I was forced to jump in and go.

David and I headed to the new tea shop. My mother and David had spent countless hours opening our second location. They didn't know much about the permits and licensing that went behind opening a café, so they opened it as a retail location.

When we pulled up, I saw the sign on the wall. *New Secrets Tea*. It was nothing like I imagined, but it was the most beautiful place I had ever seen. The merchandise was lined up along the walls, there was a huge screen that displayed our selection, the lights were bright, and the smell was delectable. I was so proud of what they had done. I felt like a mama bear who had just witnessed her cubs catch their first prey. I couldn't have been more grateful.

A small piece of me was saddened when I realized that almost all of what they had designed was going to have to change, but I thought they would be okay with it. I was wrong.

What do you mean you're changing things? Do you have any idea how much work we put into this? Do you know how much money we spent? Do you know how many hours we spent sweating over inventory to keep your dream alive? And now you want to just come in here like a tornado and rip everything up? Who do you think you are? Are you mad? You didn't even consult with us to know how we feel?

There was so much heat, and to be honest, I understood it all. I felt terrible, and it was the last emotion I wanted anyone to feel, especially these two, but the truth of the matter was we were not going to survive that location as just a retail spot. Numbers said that, not me! People were excited we finally had a brick and mortar they didn't have to fly to get to, and sales needed to include cups of tea and food items. It was our only chance of longevity as a company at this location. I had to make an executive decision, and unfortunately it left me solo.

David didn't feel appreciated for all he had done, including taking a loan out to keep the lights on, a fact I learned about when searching through papers. Mom felt like she had just done all this work for nothing, which had mostly to do with her ego and not having the control she'd had over the last few months. Truth was, none of that was true. I wasn't trying to take over. In fact, if all went well I would have gladly taken a seat and let them do their thing, but after further review of paperwork and financials, I saw that the current state would give us about two months before we would be shutting down, so I had decided to close the doors at Remington for a revamp. I had about 27 days to get things together. I only had this long because funds were not going to cover doors being closed much longer. I didn't really understand what happened to all the money, but honestly, unless it was stashed in a warehouse somewhere, which we all knew it wasn't, it really didn't matter.

I tried contacting Jamal to break down what had happened and to figure out how we could predict the future. I still wasn't getting any response. All my messages were going in green. I was in disbelief because we had just spent so many hours talking on 15 minute clips for the last few months. 4166 minutes to be exact. There was a small piece of me thinking that we would probably get together. I mean, my marriage wasn't exactly panning out, and he had been with me through the lowest part of my life, providing me the comfort I was looking for in my husband.

He's a busy man and he also didn't know I was home, so he's probably in a place with bad service, I told myself.

Turns out, I was blocked. Donna showed me a pic he had posted of him and my cousin in Aruba hugged up. I guess he *didn't* have service but not for the reason I thought. Donna didn't know the relationship we had developed, so her response to the shock on my face was truly concerning. Instantly I found myself fighting back tears. My heart was in my toes once again.

What a reality to return to. My mom hated my guts because she felt I'd taken away her last chance of redemption, David didn't even want to have sex with me, and the man that I had just spent months building a relationship with, who I was quite frankly ready to leave my husband for, had apparently dumped me—for my cousin. Yikes!

At that very moment, Michael and Michelle came bursting through the doors. The pain sat in my chest, right next to the joy I got from being able to hold them at will.

I soon discovered we were dealing with some PTSD between the two of them. Whenever I left the view of Michael, he would cry uncontrollably and ask if I was coming back. Michelle had a thing about loud noises. I found that out after closing my closet door too quickly. There was a loud bang, and I heard her screaming. When I peeked around the corner, she was under the table shaking in fear of someone bursting through our door again. It was so sad, but we were working through it as gently as possible.

Business was alive but suffering, finances were missing with no explanation, my marriage was heading for the rocks, not to mention, my side entanglement had just backfired in my face. My children were traumatized, and I was a minute away from being homeless because my mom was now moving to New York. I couldn't get an apartment or job for that matter due to being a 'criminal.' I owned all of one outfit and 3 pairs of underwear, and I was in so much debt due to moves I had no idea were taking place. I found myself trying to pull it together, but with every new thought that popped up there was less and less air entering my lungs. The room was spinning, and my chest grew tight. I was on the verge of having an anxiety attack. My new reality was so overwhelming.

As I was trying my hardest to catch a breath, Donna caught me heaving. She helped me to a chair and was mumbling something.

This moment brought me back to a moment in labor when I was on the verge of passing out. My mom was in the corner labor breathing for me, my mother-in-law was in the corner speaking in tongues, and my sister was telling me to listen to her voice. Everyone meant well, I'm sure, but it was causing so much confusion and anxiety, I didn't know how to respond. So I did what I know best: I told everyone to be quiet. I got quiet myself and began to focus on my breath.

This is only a moment in time. Pain is momentary, focus on your breath. IN... OUT... INNNN... OUTTTT.... One minute later, my first child was here.

In my moments of attack, I saw her little face, wide blue eyes, and I was almost certain she smiled at me before she began to cry.

When I closed my eyes, trying to find my bearings, I reflected on that very moment. I saw her bright eyes staring right back at me. A wave of peace came over me.

"It will be okay. I have weathered the toughest of storms. This WILL NOT be the reason I fail."

"I will never leave nor forsake you. Seek ye first the Kingdom of God" - God

I had made a promise, not only to myself, but to God. Nothing or Nobody would precede my time with God and family. All responsibilities would be prayerfully balanced. I said I would be gentle with myself when it came to meeting certain expectations. I would no longer beat myself up, nor would I ever allow someone else to have that power.

I prayed and prepared for a mindset makeover. I stopped to really evaluate.

I've been hurt.

I've been beaten.

I've been abused.

I've been poisoned (quite literally).

I've been used.

I've been alone.

I've been afraid.

I was broken and I was broke, but I was not lonely. Alone and lonely are not the same. One describes your physical position. The other is spiritual.

I have never been lonely.

Every single situation I've found myself in.

Every single step I've taken.

God had me.

I'd come up for air and realized there really is nothing to fear. Even in the darkest of times, there is a light inside, and if I can just focus on it, I can and will shine brighter than any darkness I could ever know.

So here I was finding myself in a room with people I knew loved me. I found myself smiling, but I'm sure I looked crazy. One minute I was having a mini heart attack and the next, I was smiling. If I was on the outside looking in, "bipolar" would have been my first guess.

Luckily, it was just my children and Donna, so I was safe from being judged. I caught eyes with her, and her eyebrows were so far up her forehead her eyes were going to pop out. We both burst out laughing. We laughed so hard my sides hurt, and tears fell from my eyes. The more I laughed, the lighter I felt. I didn't realize it then, but I was releasing. I had so much inside that once I started, I couldn't stop. My laugh was almost unstoppable and most definitely authentic.

One thing I've learned through this experience. When something happens, feel it. Let yourself go through the emotions. Rid your body of the pain. Empty your soul of shame. Then when your tears dry, take a few breaths and realize… "Everything little thing is going to be all right!" —the realest Bob Marley quote there is.

A few minutes later when all chuckling ceased, I returned to my thought of to-dos. Only this time, I could see more clearly. The list hadn't changed and neither had the vision, but my view did. I took the list, took an even bigger breath, and sat down.

I prayed, because I'm something like a warrior now. I'm not exactly sure what I said, but it went a little something like: (*feel free to say it with me*)

"Dear God,

I need Your help. Speak clearly to me so I know each step I take is ordained by you. You know the desires of my heart, but Your will be done. Help me today, Father. Guide me. Lead me. Use me. Order my steps. I cannot do this without You, I WILL NOT do this without You. I NEED YOU.

Amen"

I then took the list and broke it all down, each to-do item. I wrote down every single step I would need to take to complete each task. I organized, prioritized, and strategized. I had almost doubled my list by time I was done, but now I had a plan.

Little did I know, this list had become the 8 Steps to a Successful Wellness Based Business. I thought about all the "success we had before." How did we get there? What worked and didn't work? What should we repeat, and where do we need to improve? I even thought about my "failures." How did I get them? How do I avoid a repeat? How can I make this process something that I can achieve excellence in over and over again, and even share with others? I reviewed old and new things, conversations, numbers, data, processes, everything you can think of. I broke it down to just eight attainable steps. But I needed to make sure this worked, and I had less than 25 days to get it done.

OM: THE SELF WITHIN

"When I gladden my heart, I awaken the energy of gratitude. This energy uplifts and expands me. By opening my heart, I can feel gratitude deeply. Gratitude shifts the moment by shifting me. Nothing around me changes; but I change."

- Natalie Antoinette -

Amadhi

ULTIMATE BLISS

*T*HESE NEXT FEW weeks were nothing easy. I'm not sure why I thought my return home would mean that the world had changed. I mean, I did! What was wrong with the world?

I began to implement the 8 steps to a successful business.

STEP 1 - MINDSET MAKEOVER.

You have to get your mind in the correct space to receive success. Your past does not have to determine your future. We all have the ability to change our lives. We can be, do, and have exactly what we wish, if our mind will let us.

STEP - KNOW YOUR WHY

What is your purpose and reason for this action? There needs to be one, and it needs to be clear to you. Why? Because there are going to be rocky moments, as you will soon see, and if your why is not clear to you, you WILL throw in the towel. It's inevitable, and that's fine. It's how you respond to this moment that matters.

STEP 3 - KNOW YOUR BRAND PROMISE

What is the problem I am solving for my customers? What do they need help with and how can I help?

STEP 4 - GET CLEAR ON YOUR MARKET

Who exactly am I serving? A lot of times, we want to serve one community or group, but in actuality, our service best serves someone else. Who is that and how do I effectively reach them?

STEP 5 - DEVISE A PLAN

Not just any plan. One that works for me. That starts right where I am and takes me to the next step. What are my step-by-step action items to be delivered?

STEP 6 -TAKE ACTION

Well, this is simple enough. No point in having a plan if you are not going to take the action. This step is so much easier when Step 4 is completed with real life in mind.

STEP 7 - MARKETING

This is the part I used to get hung up on. I felt like I needed to have a certain number of followers, or likes on my pictures. But that's not the case. In fact, after being absent for so long, it was almost as if I had to start completely over. You know how that algorithm goes. But the truth is, you can have 100 followers and still be wildly successful. You can have 100,000 followers and no success. In fact, I just read an article about an influencer with over 1 million followers who couldn't sell 10 shirts. What's important is not the quantity but the quality of your following. Wherever you are, start there and build to your appropriate audience. Everything else is fluff and does not increase your bank balance. Trust me, I know.

STEP 8 - DEVELOP A TEAM

This does not mean you need to go hire a bunch of people. Plus I wasn't in the position to do so. This just means you need to understand the different roles of your company. Furthermore, it really means you need a support team. Someone or a group of someones who are going through what you are going through. People who understand your plight because they have been there or are going through it as well. This can often come in a FB group, through a coach, or things of the like. This is one of the most important steps. A support team can also help you during those *"This ain't for me"* moments that WE ALL experience.

With that in mind, I got down to business.

Spoiler alert: Everything that could go wrong did.

Paperwork was so screwed, and there were no funds to fix it. I spent the majority of the next few days in between state buildings, talking to people who had been at their jobs for over 20 years and still had no clue how to solve ordinary problems. That was a frustration all in itself, but I moved past it.

Anytime a negative thought or emotion came about, and lord knows that was quite often, "Eh, could be worse. This is such a blessing" would automatically come from my mouth. It got to a point where my own mother asked if I was going to use that for the rest of my life. I said yes!

I did what I could do on the side to make extra money: meal prep, yoga classes, other odds and ends to pull together enough to get us started. I had raised a little under $3K in just a matter of 20 days. Every single dime went back into the business. I used this money to make table and chair purchases, paid for permits, and got us more inventory.

Now some may not agree that this should have been my first move, considering I didn't have a dime to my name. But I believed in this, I believed in me. And more importantly, I don't believe God would have given me this vision if I wasn't supposed to have it. I had asked God to provide, to show me the way to go and to give me the courage to move. How silly would I be to ask for something and not trust that He will answer? *Why even ask, right?*

So yes, I wasn't sure how or when exactly I would be back on my feet, especially with all the new problems presenting themselves, but I knew one thing for sure and two things for certain: God Got Me!

Saturday, April 5th, 2019 rolled around.

I was nervous and anxious all at once. It wasn't completely done the way I envisioned, but 9am hit, lights cut on, and doors were opened.

The bar had been made into a rose gold marble countertop with a woodgrain base. The retail wall was lit with bright attractive lights to display all the well manufactured glass jars. The containers with tea and a variety of herbs lined the back of the bar like alcohol. In the corner was a meditation section with hanging lights and a scented Buddha head. The outer beauty section, made of tea baths, was lined with different salts and sugars for each customer to custom make scrubs as they desired.

The dining area allowed for some to sit and enjoy, while others took some to go. From 9:30am until about 8pm, the doors were coming off the hinges. I saw so many people who I wasn't even aware knew about the event. Friends from the airport, high school and college friends, neighbors, out-of-staters, White people, Black people, green people, really just a bit of everyone. I never gave so many hugs in one day. I was even hugging complete strangers.

I was in complete shock when I looked up and saw Jamal. He stood in the back with official "New Secrets Tea" gear. He'd even invited a few friends, which was nice. My heart warmed at knowing he cared enough to support me and show his face, but my mind wouldn't forget what I was feeling. I showed no emotion on the outside. He did make a few purchases, shared how proud of me he was, and gave me the biggest hug, in which I almost melted in his arms. That was the last time I saw Jamal.

By the end of the night, the majority of inventory was gone, and I was dog tired. My niece, nephews, and mom stayed back to help clean while I counted today's earnings. We made well over 5K. A miracle in itself.

David never showed.

Just then, a white lady came in. We were technically closed for the day, but since we were still there, I welcomed her in. She had a pie in her hand. She said her name was Sarah and she wanted to welcome us to the neighborhood. She wasn't a coffee drinker and was excited when she learned we would be joining her on her block. She expressed she made pie because that's all she knew how to bake and explained she would tell all her friends to come out. After parting ways, my family left behind her.

I sat quietly in the new location, staring at the delicious looking apple pie. Now, I did contemplate not eating it because, well, I didn't know the lady. I had already been tricked once, and I didn't want to be had twice. But I took a knife and slowly cut it anyway.

"Eh. It could be worse," I chuckled.

It was as if all the build-up I had in me all day just oozed out of my pores. I was just dripping with gratitude.

We did it. We'd pulled it off. I was smiling in a shop that I was the CEO of. I didn't do it alone, but I had actually pulled it off. The devil had won the battle, but I had won the war.

Fast forward to a year later. The children have worked through their "PTSD." I think the new problem we may be facing is entitlement. My daughter told me she doesn't want her strawberries diced up, and she hasn't liked it since she was a child *insert eye roll* while my son just wants to eat everything his little hands can grab.

Since implementing the eight steps, business has been wildly successful. So much so, I have started two other businesses with the same method and have now helped over 40 other wellness-based companies start and grow their businesses to six figures, a real accomplishment in my book. I only wish someone had shown me the ropes like I am doing now, because there is room for ALL of us to win. Plus when the ego is removed, you will notice that your win is actually my win. Imagine if I had given up.

I NEVER GAVE UP!

My friendships are all great. My circle is a lot smaller than before, but energy is vibrating high. They say your vibe attracts your tribe. Although this is a cool saying, it really is the truth. It's all about the energy exchange. Now... if you don't match my vibe, there's no need to argue or try to change you. I don't even have any ill feeling. I simply identify it and make sure I protect my aura, whatever that may look like. Some people have limited access, some have none at all. It is what it is. Life keeps moving, and I'm going to make sure I spend my time in a positive place.

My marriage.... Well, this is the biggest test of them all. I mean, just think about the little bit you know from this book alone. We weren't facing things like going through your DM (not that that isn't a real problem), but we had some real demons to face. Going to jail, let alone together, brought out some real battles. Battles that we are fighting every day. Will we make it out on the other side? Well, only God knows that real answer, but we are trying. We both value family very much; however, there has been a lot of hurt and pain in the process, and the important thing is that we both HEAL. That is where the real magic happens.

Epilogue

So here we are, on the other side of a very traumatic experience. Sometimes it's hard to see the fire through the smoke, as Grandma always said, but looking back I can see the very things that helped get me through the troubled times.

First it starts with the mind rituals.

- Starting wherever you are and dealing with your stuff. If you experience something, even if it's little, you deserve to deal with it.
- Writing things down could potentially save your life. It allows you to connect with your inner self, where the true You lives. Connect and never let go.
- Learn to be grateful for everything, even when you feel grateful for nothing.

Then start with some spiritual rituals as well. You can't control how others treat you, but you can control how you respond. Protect your inner peace, by any means necessary.

In retrospect, if there was anything I learned from my experiences, it's:

- *PUT GOD FIRST.*

There was a time that we were doing so well in the business that I felt like I had made it all happen. Of course I knew God was the one responsible for my success, but I never said anything about it. While sitting in the darkest space of my life, I realized I may not have committed this crime, but there was a reason for my sit.

Now... there is not a day that I will let pass that I don't thank Him OUT LOUD for all that He has done. Even when someone comes and buys a $5 infuser, I thank Him. Or when the children come in and poke me in the eye to wake me up for breakfast.

- THE ATTITUDE OF GRATITUDE

This has made me an overall happier person. The things I once never thought about, like having a blanket to sleep with, I cherish like nobody's business. Being able to eat when I want or having hot water at will. All luxuries I never even thought twice about.

- PROTECT YOUR ENERGY

Not all my relationships made it through the storm. And some were very shocking, particularly my cousin, seeing how we had always been inseparable.

But the weight of the world is not for us to carry, and I was in a phase in my life that all the love I had given should be reciprocated.

Which leads me to my next lesson:

- *Love and have respect for yourself first.*

I love myself enough to recognize the different pieces of me. *Cue "Pieces of Me" by Ashley Simpson*

No but seriously, some pieces we know we need to improve on like how to communicate effectively with people, and some pieces that just make you YOU! I discovered some old pieces I once loved, but somewhere neglected it along the way, i.e. dancing. And then there were newer things that I didn't want to admit (i.e. I'm a lot more like my mother than I thought) but have learned to embrace it all.

Either way, there were pieces of me that I couldn't shake, and there would be no way in hell someone else would love all these good pieces unless I accepted them myself. Knowing that, there's nothing that anyone could say to make me think otherwise. There is something so magical about the understanding that comes with true self-awareness and self-acceptance. It truly is Power all in itself.

And none of that is meant in a conceited way, but in a voice of confidence and appreciation. I always thought of Power with a negative connotation. But the actual definition is "To have right or authority that is given or delegated to a person or body."

For so long, I gave that power to other people, seeking approval, questioning my motherhood, doubting my beliefs, but I realized its currency or value. I no longer give that away! I possess the authority over myself—outside of God of course. But no man, or woman for that matter, can take from me what God has given me.

I saw myself in the most naked form and had to come to terms with the dark to find my way back to the light. With that said, I no longer accept energies around me that are draining. I am no longer willing to be invited into a partnership that only takes, while I'm left empty.

Because my last lesson was about time.

- *Time is a Valuable Resource.*

We have so little of it in the grand scheme of things, and it's literally the only thing you cannot get back. I am no longer willing to waste time. If this time is not benefiting me or causing me to grow, or if this time is not helping someone else to grow, this is not time well spent.

I make time for ME, something I know we forget too often, especially as a mother. But this is not negotiable any longer. If I do not spend the time filling myself back up, I will be in no condition to carry the family as expected. Nobody wins! So I make sure I get a day of the week where I do things that I want to do (usually it's some variation of pampering…. or sleeping, that's a thing too).

Here is a short list of some physical ways I show up for myself:
1. Taking a bath (not a shower) - so simple and yet so profound
2. Praying and meditating, in that order
3. Writing letters and thank you notes, to others and to myself
4. Drinking tea daily
5. Traveling often, near and far, for the day or for the week
6. Dancing like nobody's watching. Music feeds the soul.
7. Doing yoga, exercising and eating right … *or eating the donut, whichever my heart desires that day.*
8. Buying myself flowers, or picking them from the garden, both work.

9. Reading
10. Calling people I love but don't speak to as often as I should
11. Listening to the sound of rain
12. Updating my skin and hair care routines
13. Taking a break when I need one, stopping to focus on my breath for a full minute
14. Burning sage and essential oils. *I really do smell like nag champa incense. haha*
15. Treating myself to froyo
16. Being myself, regardless of who may not agree

Some may think that this experience was a loss of time. Maybe even a waste. I say it's a little of both in your perspective. But think about it; had it *not* been for this experience, I *would* have lost time... with my children, my family, my Self!

Because of this, I now know who I am. I know where I stand. Because of this, I value myself like nobody's business. Truth is, it isn't anybody's business but mine. Once you know your self-worth, you can then value those around you, making me more selective with my energy exchange. It's the best feeling in the world to have the power and freedom of letting go of the ego, finding a true power from within.

So with time being your most expensive currency, how are you going to spend it? It's time to create your own Shiny, Joyful, Inspired, HELL YESS life. It all starts with the mindset shift.

Here are a few prompts I used in my journal. Try these out:
1. Today, here is what I feel in my heart...
2. Today, here are ten things I like about myself.
3. Today, I am grateful for this very small thing that happened...
4. Dearest Journal, here is what I want people to say about me when I'm not present...
5. If nothing else mattered—not money, kids, jobs, or expectations, my dream would look like...
6. Today, I set my intention to act with...

I hope this book has inspired you in some way to get up and try. Maybe it's given you a spark to keep pushing for that vision, or maybe to leap for the dream. If nothing else, I hope you got a little smile from reading it. And I hope you can take away this very lesson:

Know that regardless of where you come from, or what you have gone through, if you take the TIME, you will realize that all you need lies within. But you must Be Still to hear it. My question to you…

How will you spend your most valuable asset in life—TIME?

I appreciate you for taking this journey with me, and I look forward to hearing some of your Purpose through Pain moments.

Bonus

Learning how to love ourselves is often the most transformative thing we can accomplish, and it doesn't have to take a lifetime to learn.

Self-Love is a core component of true happiness. If we are unable to see the beauty and strength in ourselves, it will be hard to see it in others, or better yet, for others to see it in us as well.

Learning to love ourselves is one of the most important skills we can master here on earth. In a world that constantly tells you that you are not enough, cultivating self-love is a radical act of self establishment, expression, and discovery that allows you to take your own place on this stage of life.

WHAT IS SELF-LOVE?

We tend to think of self-love as a state of mind that makes us feel good and content.

While that is true, it's more than that.

It's an appreciation for yourself that extends far past the superficial and into your core. It's dynamic and encompasses all behaviors, thoughts, and reactions in a way that encourages growth and a celebration of strength.

When we learn to love ourselves, we empower a part of us that will make better decisions, and bolster our physical, spiritual, and psychological development.

Mastering the art of Self-Love takes time and hard work, but it brings with it truly incredible lessons that can turn your life around for the better.

BENEFITS OF SELF-LOVE

- Seeing to your needs - When you don't love yourself, it's easy to overlook your own needs and trade them for someone else's.
- Building Resilience - Loving ourselves increases our confidence and helps us get better dealing with adversity
- Gaining Fulfillment - Self-Love empowers us to accept our lives and the situations we find ourselves in and it also empowers us to realize that we alone are the source of our own happiness and fulfillment in life.
- Healthier Habits - Learning how to love yourself on the inside has a funny way of manifesting itself on the out.

THE 7 DAY OM CHALLENGE

By adapting these very simple steps, one at a time and staying consistent with it, it helped to grow my Self-Appreciation. In just 7 days, you can start cultivating the self-love you need to thrive, but you have got to open up your mind.... and your heart!

DAY 1: MINDFUL MEDITATION

Mindful meditation can best be described as a mental training process that allows you to unlock the true power and potential from within. This may look a little different for each of us. Start small, with 5 mins and increase it over time. If you have a thought, accept it and move forward. Practice this enough and you will get to a place of clarity, but be patient, this may not happen the first 3 times.

DAY 2: COMING FIRST

Move from setting the right mindset, to learning how to put yourself and your emotions first. When we don't truly love ourselves like we should, we start to view ourselves as unworthy, and that's when you start to fall out of place.

DAY 3: ACCEPTING YOURSELF

If you're struggling to love yourself, chances are you are also struggling with accepting who you are and where you are in life. Self-Love and Self-Acceptance go hand in hand.

DAY 4: LEARN HOW TO SELF-CARE

Self-care Sunday doesn't look the same for everyone. Maybe it's writing in a journal, maybe it's exercising or doing yoga, maybe it's cleaning the house, whatever feeds your soul, do that! It doesn't have to require the entire day, and it doesn't have to be something drastic and hard to accomplish. Whatever it is, make it a part of your routine.

DAY 5: REDEFINING HAPPINESS

Though it may seem hard to grasp at first, Happiness is a choice. And it's a choice that we can make every single day. You can choose to be happy or you can choose to be sad, but we have to love and respect ourselves enough to understand that.

DAY 6: PRACTICE GRATITUDE

One of the biggest contributing factors to our continued unhappiness is a loss of gratitude. The idea that I will be happy when……

Learning how to be grateful for everything you currently have will not only bolster our sense of contentment, but also a great way to combat the hopelessness and anxiety we often feel.

Find a quiet place and take some time to write down 10 things that you are truly grateful for

DAY 7: WRITE A LOVE LETTER TO YOURSELF

The biggest problem many of us face in the modern world is the lack of love we feel around us. Many of us look for love elsewhere and seek external validation for something that comes from within. If we want to feel love passionately and unconditionally, we must first love ourselves that way, and we can start with something as simple as writing a letter to ourselves

Nobody knows you as well as you know yourself. Talk about your strengths, your beauty, your best qualities. Now is the time to boast. Let it all out and don't hold back.

Learning to love yourself may be one of the hardest skills we learn, but it's the most rewarding and fulfilling accomplishment and truly should be a goal for life.

Start this journey with a little mindful meditation and stay true to this process. The first few days will be the hardest. But if you stick with it, it will not only change your life, but you will wonder how you ever lived without it.

Take the journey and tag #TheOmChallenge and @ItsNatalieAntoinette so we can share the journey with you.

With much love and light
- NatalieAntoinette

www.ingramcontent.com/pod-product-compliance
Lightning Source LLC
Chambersburg PA
CBHW071451070526
44578CB00001B/303